はじめのいっぽ
First Steps in Japanese

はじめのいっぽ
First Steps in Japanese

谷口すみ子・萬浪絵理
稲子あゆみ・萩原弘毅　共著

スリーエーネットワーク

3A Corporation
Shoei Bldg., 6-3, Sarugaku-cho 2-chome, Chiyoda-ku, Tokyo 101-0064, Japan

First published in Japan by 3A Corporation 1995

ISBN4-88319-041-2 C0081
Printed in Japan

はじめに：この本を作るとき、考えたこと

　どんなに短期間の滞在でも、その国のことばを全く知らないのと、少しでも知っているのとでは、便利さだけではなく、心の触れ合いのしかたがずいぶんと違ってくるのではないでしょうか。何か月、何年と滞在する人にとってはなおさらのことです。しかし、現在、日本には、日本語を学びたくとも学ぶ機会のない人たちが大勢います。正式の日本語教育を受ける機会がない人たちも、当たり前のことですが、人・もの・情報に自由に接近する権利を持っています。

　この本は、そうした自分の生活の場をよりよくしたいと思っている人や、学びたくとも正規の学習の場のない人たちのために作りました。また、初級の日本語は一応習ったものの、実際の会話ができないという人が、1人で、もしくは、教室で先生とともに使うこともできます。

　この本を編むにあたって次のような点に留意しました。

　現実には、多様な日本語が飛び交っています。したがって会話文を過度に単純化せず、現実を反映するよう心がけました。文法的にも、規範性にとらわれるよりも、意図・意思を少ない語彙表現で何とか伝達できるよう配慮しました。例えば、「この電車は新宿へ行きますか」という文は初級教科書では必ず取り上げられていますが、現実の場面では、「この電車、新宿、行きますか」という言い方をすることがあります。この本では後者の言い方を取り上げ、文法ノートで前者のようないわば規範的な言い方を紹介し、文法学習の一助となるようにしました。

　また、従来の教材では、日本人が一方的に質問あるいは指示を与え、学習者がそれにこたえる場面、状況が多い気がします。しかし学ぶということは、特にコミュニケーションの手段を学ぶということは、現実を変え、自分の世界を広げるという意味を持つと思います。

　この本では、日本社会で生活していて、何が問題なのか、どう解決すればいいのかを考える一助となるような素材の提供ができたらと考えました。

　そのためまず日本に来た人々にとってどのような場面が必要なのか洗い出しました。その際、単に用を足すだけの会話（例：銀行、買い物）だけではなく、プライベート・タイムで必要な場面（例：宗教、娯楽）も考えました。また実用的場面であっても、その過程で、現実に問題になるのはどのような場面なのか特定し、教材にしました（例：駅では、切符を買う場面よりは、プラットフォームで入ってきた電車が目的地に行くかどうか、近くの人に尋ねることができる。また、買い物では、買うときだけが問題なのではなく、欲しいものがどこにあるのか、どう行くのかといった全過程を検討した）。

　場面別会話集は語彙・表現の羅列になってしまいがちです。昔からのことわざに、「一匹の魚を与えるは一時の恵み、釣り方を教えるは、一生の恵み」とありますが、この本も、釣った魚（語彙・表現）を与えるよりは、魚の釣り方（問題解決の方法）を、釣りをしながら身につけてもらえればと思って作りました。このテキストを通じて学習者の皆さんが新たな問題に遭遇したときに周りの日本人と話し合いながら、問題を解決していく方法を学んでくだされば著者一同、本望です。

　なお、この本の出版に際して、財団法人海外技術者研修協会東京研修センター春原憲一郎氏に、多くの助言と協力を頂きました。ここに感謝の意を表します。

5

1995年3月
著　者

凡　例

Ⅰ. この本の構成

1. 準備学習…日本語の音節、日本語の表記・日本語の発音・アクセント・イントネーション、日本語文法概論

2. コラム…日本語の体系的な知識を得たいとき、読んでください。
   あいさつ、数字・数詞、助数詞、時刻、時間、ストラテジーのまとめ、年月日、丁寧体と普通体、疑問詞のまとめに分かれています。

3. 本文…全部で15課あります。
   各課の構成。
   ① 会話例（漢字かな＋ローマ字＋英語訳）
   ② 文法ノート（この本を全部勉強すると初級文法前半がほぼ学べます）
   ③ 練習
   ④ 福袋（知っていると便利な文字、関連情報、関連語彙から発展活動、異文化交流について考える問題まで、楽しくためになる情報の宝の山です。なお、異文化交流の問題は、初級の日本語で答えるのは難しいかもしれません。その場合は、英語で話し合ってみてください。）

4. 索引…巻末には、全単語リストを載せました。

Ⅱ. 学習の進め方：今どんなことができるようになりたいですか。
例：第3課の学び方

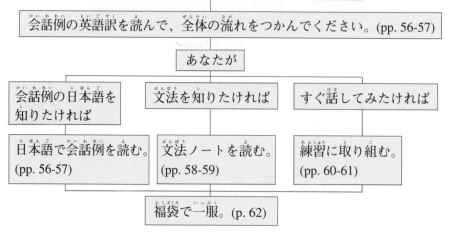

もし、あなたが1人で日本のレストランで食事をしてみたいと思ったら、
→「第3課 食べる Taberu Eating」

会話例の英語訳を読んで、全体の流れをつかんでください。(pp. 56-57)

あなたが

| 会話例の日本語を知りたければ | 文法を知りたければ | すぐ話してみたければ |

| 日本語で会話例を読む。(pp. 56-57) | 文法ノートを読む。(pp. 58-59) | 練習に取り組む。(pp. 60-61) |

福袋で一服。(p. 62)

注1：会話例の中に、*str.1-1, p. 106* という表示があります。これは、ストラテジーのまとめ（pp. 106-107）を参照するためのもので、このストラテジーについての解説が得られます。

注2：文法について疑問があったら、コラムを参照してください。

Preface

What was considered in making this textbook

However short your stay in a foreign country might be, it would make a big difference whether or not you had some knowledge of the language of the country. After all, language has an important role not only for communication purposes but for allowing us to cross a divide and share culture. The knowledge of the language becomes more important when you are to stay in the country for a longer period of time. The truth is, however, there are now in Japan many people from abroad that have no opportunities to study the Japanese language formally despite their desire to do so. Needless to say, those with no such opportunities are also endowed with the right to gain free access to people, goods and information.

This book is intended to help those who wish to know more about the environment around them, enabling them to lead a more comfortable existence in Japan, as well as those who are not able to receive formal Japanese language lessons. It is also possible, for those who have already attended an elementary course of the language but cannot practically speak it, to use this book for self-study or in a language class under the guidance of a teacher.

The following considerations were given to this textbook in the process of its writing.

In reality, many different types of Japanese language are spoken and heard. It therefore doesn't make sense, from a practical viewpoint, to oversimplify Japanese conversations for the students who read the textbook; rather, the variety of expressions encountered in the real world should be incorporated in it. The rules of grammar were not strictly adhered to. Instead, efforts were made to show ways to convey one's feelings and intentions using a limited vocabulary. For example, a typical expression found in a Japanese textbook for beginners is 'Kono densha wa Shinjuku e ikimasu ka (Does this train go to Shinjuku?).' What one often hears, though, is 'Kono densha, Shinjuku, ikimasu ka.' This textbook takes up the expressions of the latter type, while introducing under the heading of **Grammatical Notes** the former type, i.e., formal expressions, in order to help students learn about grammar as well.

Generally, Japanese textbooks and teaching materials tend to have Japanese people asking questions and making requests of the otherwise passive foreigners. However, we believe that learning something new and being equipped with the means of communication will change the student's life and widen the area of his or her activities. Consequently, this textbook tries to help the student identify the causes of, and find solutions to, problems encountered in his/her life in Japan.

With such views in mind, situations were sorted out where foreigners in Japan are normally placed. In addition to basic words and phrases that are indispensable for them to get by in this country, such as those for shopping or making themselves understood at a bank, conversations for private-life situations, including those related to religions and entertainment, were introduced in this book. Attempts were also made to set up some specific situations that might cause foreigners some difficulties. For instance, problems faced by them at a station are not so much with buying tickets but rather with asking a Japanese on the platform whether an incoming train will take them to their destination. In shopping, it is essential for people to know how much should be paid, but they should also be able to ask where they can find what they are looking for or how they can get there.

A textbook of conversations for many different situations more often than not looks like a list of vocabulary and expressions. As an old adage says, if you give a man a fish, he will eat for a day, while if you teach him how to fish, he will eat for all his life. This textbook is meant to show students how to fish so that they can fish by themselves, not to give them fish that have already been caught (vocabulary and expressions). Those who were involved in producing this textbook would be more than delighted if readers could learn, through this textbook, to tackle and solve problems by talking with the Japanese people surrounding them.

We owe a great debt of thanks to Mr. Ken'ichiro Haruhara, a Japanese language teacher of the Association for Overseas Technical Scholarship, who provided valuable advice and support with the publication of this textbook.

The authors

Explanatory Notes

Ⅰ. The Structure of This Book

1. **Japanese Syllabaries, The Japanese Writing System, Pronunciation, Accent, Intonation, Introduction to Japanese Grammar**: Please read these sections before starting to study with this book.

2. **Language Focus**: This section should be read when systematic knowledge of the Japanese language is necessary. It includes **Greetings and Set Phrases, Numerals, Counting, Time Expressions, Periods of Time, Summary of Strategies, Years, Months and Days, Polite and Plain Styles** and **Summary of Interrogative Words**.

3. **Main Text**: There are 15 lessons in total, each of which consists of the following:
   ① **Dialogues** (Chinese characters and kana-syllabary + romanized letters + English translations)
   ② **Grammatical Notes** (When this textbook is entirely covered, students will have virtually mastered the first half of elementary Japanese grammar.)
   ③ **Exercises**
   ④ **Fukubukuro** (This contains valuable pieces of information, including useful characters, associated vocabulary, supplementary information, extended activities, and cross-cultural issues. If it is difficult for you to answer the questions concerning cross-cultural issues using elementary Japanese, try to discuss them in English.)

4. **Index**: All the words used in this textbook are listed at the end of the volume.

Ⅱ. How to Use This Textbook - What would you like to learn now?

Example: Lesson 3

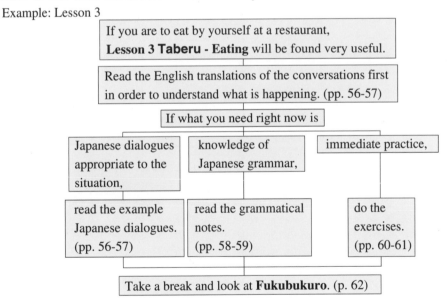

Note 1: You will find such information as *str. 1-1, p. 106* under certain words in the example dialogues. This is used to refer you to the strategies on pages 106-107.

Note 2: The **Language Focus** section will also help you get a better understanding of Japanese grammar.

Contents

Table of Contents

Title/ Dialogues	Grammatical Notes
1 Introducing Yourself Ⅰ. At a party/Asking someone's name Ⅱ. Asking someone's nationality Ⅲ. Asking someone's job	1. ～は～です。 ～ wa ～ desu. 2. ～か。 ～ ka. 3. はい（ええ）、～です。 Hai (Ee), ～ desu. 4. いいえ、～では（じゃ）ありません。 　 Iie, ～ dewa (ja) arimasen. 5. ～さん ～-san 6. ～は？ ～ wa? 7. ～の～ ～ no ～
2 Shopping Ⅰ. At a supermarket/Asking where to find 　 something Ⅱ. At a kiosk/Asking the price Ⅲ. At the front desk of a hotel/Asking if 　 something is available	1. ～はここ／そこ／あそこです。 　 ～ wa koko/soko/asoko desu. 2. ～は～の前／後ろ／近くです。 　 ～ wa ～ no mae/ushiro/chikaku desu. 3. ～（を）ください。 ～ (o) kudasai. 4. ～はありますか。 ～ wa arimasu ka. 5. いくらですか。 Ikura desu ka.
3 Eating Ⅰ. At a restaurant/Attracting attention Ⅱ. Ordering Ⅲ. Asking about one's order	1. これ／それ／あれは～です。 　 Kore/Sore/Are wa ～ desu. 2. ひとつ、ふたつ、みっつ…hitotsu, futatsu, mittsu 3. ～、お願いします。 ～, onegai-shimasu. 4. ～、まだですか。 ～, mada desu ka.
4 Talking Ⅰ. Talking about a wedding photo Ⅱ. Talking about one's family	1. ～歳 ～-sai 2. Adjectives 3. Avoiding topics
5 Mailing Ⅰ. At the mailing window/Mailing a letter Ⅱ. At the stamp window/Buying stamps and 　 postcards Ⅲ. At the parcel window/Mailing a parcel	1. ～でお願いします。 ～ de onegai-shimasu. 2. ～枚 ～-mai 3. ～まで～でいくらですか。 　 ～ made ～ de ikura desu ka. 4. ～まで～でどのくらいかかりますか。 　 ～ made ～ de donokurai kakarimasu ka.
6 Phoning Ⅰ. Calling a company Ⅱ. Calling a friend	1. ～さん、お願いします。 　 ～-san, onegai-shimasu. 2. ～と申しますが。 ～ to mooshimasu ga. 3. ～さん、いらっしゃいますか。 　 ～-san, irasshaimasu ka. 4. Omission of -san 5. 失礼ですが… Shitsuree desu ga… 6. 少々、お待ちください。 　 Shooshoo, o-machi kudasai. 7. もしもし。 Moshimoshi. 8. じゃ、結構です。 Ja, kekkoo desu.

🖊 **Exercises**	🧧 **Fukubukuro**
1. Introducing yourself 2. Confirming words 3. Making a business card + Introducing yourself 4. Confirming meaning 5. Answering questions 6. Asking a person's country	1. Katakana (name) 2. Words related to occupations and countries 3. What would you do if...? Social customs
1. Indicating position and place 2. (1) Asking location 　(2) Asking availability 3. Shopping	1. Bargain sales 2. What would you do if...you couldn't see the price? 　(Asking availability)
1. Asking what things are 2. Ordering food (1) 3. Ordering food (2) 4. Hurrying up the waiter	1. Foods and dishes 2. What would you do if...you couldn't read the menu?
1. Stating age 2. Talking about photos 3. Talking about photos of children	1. Family members 2. What would you do if...? Topics of conversation
1. Sending things 2. Buying stamps and aerograms 3. Sending parcels	1. Post office windows 2. Mailboxes 3. SAL 4. Business hours
1. Calling a friend at work 2. Calling a friend at home	1. Katakana related to the telephone 2. The Chinese character for electricity 3. Useful telephone numbers 4. What would you do if...? Customs related to telephone calls

✏️ Exercises	🧧 Fukubukuro
. Using verbs . Making questions and giving answers . Enquiring about trains/stations . Asking how many stops to a specific station . Giving reasons	1. Names of stations 2. Types of trains 3. Useful signs at a station
. Asking about films, etc. . Suggesting seeing a film . Arranging to meet	1. What would you do if...? Differences in film titles 2. Contents page of an information magazine 3. Vocabulary related to entertainment
. Making the dictionary form . Saying what you like . Saying numbers of bottles . Talking about food restrictions	1. What would you do if...? Involved in a quarrel 2. Useful words on a menu 3. Vocabulary related to bars

. Identifying phrases
. Making requests
. Sending money
	1. Extended activities
	   (1) Completing an overseas remittance form
	   (2) Business hours and closed days
	2. Useful bank signs
	3. Vocabulary related to banks

. Asking for permission . Borrowing things . Asking readings/pronunciations	1. Making friends 2. Useful factory signs
. Explaining what is wrong . Giving advice	1. Vocabulary related to hospitals 2. Hospital reception
. Asking the price 2. Asking how long 3. Making requests 4. Saying what you want 5. Saying what you don't want	1. Useful hairdressing terms 2. Useful expressions

15

Title/ Dialogues	Grammatical Notes
14 **Visiting People** Ⅰ. At the front door/Visiting your superior Ⅱ. In the entrance way/Asking dos and don'ts Ⅲ. In the living room/Paying compliments Ⅳ. Handing over a gift Ⅴ. Eating Ⅵ. Saying goodbye	1. 〜たことがあります。 〜ta koto ga arimasu. 2. 〜てみます。 〜te mimasu.
15 **Religion** Ⅰ. At work/Explaining religious customs Ⅱ. At a party/Explaining about religion	1. 〜ので 〜 node 2. 〜なければいけません。 〜nakereba ikemasen. 3. 〜てはいけません。 〜te wa ikemasen. 4. Potential form of verbs

✏️ Exercises	福 Fukubukuro
1. Talking about food 2. Asking about experience 3. Encouraging people to do things 4. Paying compliments	1. Adjectives of taste 2. What would you do if...? Wanting to leave/ Customs connected with visiting people
1. Giving reasons (1) 2. Giving reasons (2) 3. Making sentences with 'nai-form + nakereba ikemasen' 4. Making sentences with 'te-form + wa ikemasen' 5. Talking about your religion 6. Changing verbs into their potential forms	1. Names of different religions 2. What would you do if...? Religious differences

Characters in the Book

マリオ・フジモト

Mario Fujimoto Mario Fujimoto A Brazilian of Japanese origin working in a Japanese construction company. He is Mr. Tanaka's junior.

李麗紅

Ri Reekoo Li Lihong A Chinese working for a Japanese computer company. She is Ms. Sato's junior.

ロバート・ジョーンズ

Robaato Joonzu Robert Jones An American journalist who has only recently come to Japan.

田中一郎

Tanaka Ichiroo Ichiro Tanaka Mario's senior.

佐藤和子

Satoo Kazuko Kazuko Sato Ms. Li's senior.

アリ・ムサビ
Ari Musabi Ali Musabi
An Iranian working in a Japanese car factory. He is Mr. Suzuki's junior.

ナンシー・スコット
Nanshii Sukotto Nancy Scott
An Australian working in a bank.

リサ・ヤマダ
Risa Yamada Lisa Yamada
A Filipino married to a Japanese.

鈴木洋平
Suzuki Yoohee Yohei Suzuki
Ali's boss.

高橋かおり
Takahashi Kaori Kaori Takahashi
A volunteer dealing with foreigners and their problems.

Japanese Syllabaries

あア	いイ	うウ	えエ	おオ
a	i	u	e	o
かカ	きキ	くク	けケ	こコ
ka	ki	ku	ke	ko
さサ	しシ	すス	せセ	そソ
sa	shi	su	se	so
たタ	ちチ	つツ	てテ	とト
ta	chi	tsu	te	to
なナ	にニ	ぬヌ	ねネ	のノ
na	ni	nu	ne	no
はハ	ひヒ	ふフ	へヘ	ほホ
ha	hi	fu	he	ho
まマ	みミ	むム	めメ	もモ
ma	mi	mu	me	mo
やヤ	(いイ)	ゆユ	(えエ)	よヨ
ya	(i)	yu	(e)	yo
らラ	りリ	るル	れレ	ろロ
ra	ri	ru	re	ro
わワ	(いイ)	(うウ)	(えエ)	をヲ
wa	(i)	(u)	(e)	o
んン				
n				

がガ	ぎギ	ぐグ	げゲ	ごゴ
ga	gi	gu	ge	go
ざザ	じジ	ずズ	ぜゼ	ぞゾ
za	ji	zu	ze	zo
だダ	ぢヂ	づヅ	でデ	どド
da	ji	zu	de	do
ばバ	びビ	ぶブ	べベ	ぼボ
ba	bi	bu	be	bo
ぱパ	ぴピ	ぷプ	ぺペ	ぽポ
pa	pi	pu	pe	po

ひらがな hiragana	カタカナ katakana	
ローマ字 rooma-ji		

きゃキャ kya	きゅキュ kyu	きょキョ kyo
しゃシャ sha	しゅシュ shu	しょショ sho
ちゃチャ cha	ちゅチュ chu	ちょチョ cho
にゃニャ nya	にゅニュ nyu	にょニョ nyo
ひゃヒャ hya	ひゅヒュ hyu	ひょヒョ hyo
みゃミャ mya	みゅミュ myu	みょミョ myo

りゃリャ rya	りゅリュ ryu	りょリョ ryo

ぎゃギャ gya	ぎゅギュ gyu	ぎょギョ gyo
じゃジャ ja	じゅジュ ju	じょジョ jo

びゃビャ bya	びゅビュ byu	びょビョ byo
ぴゃピャ pya	ぴゅピュ pyu	ぴょピョ pyo

The following katakana, although not listed in the table of Japanese syllabaries, are used to denote words of foreign origin.

シェ she
チェ che
ツァ tsa
ツェ tse　ツォ tso
ティ ti
ファ fa　フィ fi
フェ fe　フォ fo
ジェ je
ディ di
デュ dyu

The Japanese Writing System

1. Chinese characters, Hiragana, and Katakana

These are the three different types of letters used for writing Japanese. While they are all mixed in a Japanese sentence, katakana is normally used to indicate words of foreign origin, as well as names of places and people of other countries. For the rules to be followed in writing Japanese using these three types of letters, see *Shin-Nihongo no Kiso: Japanese Kana Workbook.*

Example: 高橋 さんは マリオ さんに 会 いました。
Takahashi-san wa Mario-san ni aimashita.
Mr. Takahashi met with Mario.

═══ Chinese characters 〜〜〜 Katakana ──── Hiragana

2. Romaji

Romaji (romanization) is the system of alphabetical spelling used to transliterate Japanese. One should be careful when reading Japanese words written in Roman letters as the pronunciation might be different from standard English.

Pronunciation

aka あか eki えき
iki いき osu おす
uso うそ

Japanese phonetics consists primarily of five different vowels, that is to say, a, i, u, e, and o, and the sounds where consonants and vowels are combined (e.g., ka). The table on pages 20-21 shows the main speech sounds, all of which are pronounced at a similar length.

okaasan おかあさん
ojiisan おじいさん
yuukan ゆうかん
oneesan おねえさん
tokee とけい
otoosan おとうさん
ookii おおきい

When the two same symbols representing a vowel follow each other directly, the pronunciation of that part of the word must be slightly lengthened. The double vowel aa is pronounced like 'ar' in the English word 'bar.' If you fail to pronounce such vowels the appropriate length, the meaning of the word may become entirely different. (In this textbook, vowel letters doubled in words written in Romaji indicate that they should be pronounced as long vowels.)

tsuki つき (moon) tsuuki つうき (ventilation)
toru とる (to take) tooru とおる (to pass)

kore これ
kuruma くるま

The consonant r in ra, ri, ru, re, and ro is not pronounced like English 'r,' where the tip of the tongue is usually curled, but like 'l' at the beginning of a word or a weak 'd.'

gakusee がくせい daigaku だいがく	When the consonant g in ga, gi, gu, ge, and go comes at the beginning of a word (as in gakusee), it sounds like the 'g' in English 'garden.' When g is in the middle of a word (e.g., daigaku), its sound is very close to 'ng' in English 'sing,' although Japanese people today tend to pronounce it in the same way as 'g' in 'garden.'

The sound of n varies according to the letter that follows it.

sando さんど

N before t, d, n, r, j and z represents a sound like the 'n' [n] in 'man.'

hantai kondo honne kinri
はんたい こんど ほんね きんり

sanpo さんぽ

N before b, m and p is pronounced like 'm' [m] in 'sample.'

sanban sanmee sanpo
さんばん さんめい さんぽ

sankai さんかい

N before k and g represents a sound similar to 'ng' [ŋ] in 'sing.'

sanko mangetsu
さんこ まんげつ

san'en さんえん

When the symbol n comes before s, h, y, w and vowels or at the end of a word, it sounds more nasal and is somewhat like a vowel [N]. (With the tip of the tongue raised but not touching the roof of the mouth, the air escapes through the nasal passages.)

kanshin yonhon kon'yaku konwaku ten'in
かんしん よんほん こんやく こんわく てんいん

ippai いっぱい
motto もっと
ikkai いっかい
issai いっさい

Double consonant - When any two of the consonants p, t, k or s follow each other directly, there should be a breath taken before pronouncing the second consonant. Before pronouncing pa in ippai, keep your lips closed for an instant in the middle of pronouncing the p. If a double consonant is mistakenly pronounced as a single one, the meaning of the word may be completely changed.

kasai かさい (fire) kassai かっさい (applause)
moto もと (former) motto もっと (more)

suki すき
kusuri くすり
kihon きほん

Voiceless vowel - A vowel like i or u between such voiceless consonants as k, s, t, p, and h is whispered. The same holds true for u in desu and masu, except in relaxed situations, when the pronunciation of u is voiced and lengthened.

suki kusuri kihon desu
すき くすり きほん です

Accent

a|me あ|め (candy)
a|me あめ (rain)

Unlike English, where accent is given to a syllable by stress or loudness, accent in Japanese is normally in terms of relative pitches. A change in accent may make the meaning of the word entirely different.

Intonation

A declarative sentence normally ends with a flat (→) or falling intonation (↘), while interrogative sentences end with a rising intonation (↗). In spoken Japanese, sentences are sometimes left unfinished. If this occurs with a question, a rising pitch is often used to indicate that it is a question. In this book such incomplete questions are indicated with a question mark.

横浜？どこですか。 Yokohama? Doko desu ka. Yokohama? Where is that?

Introduction to Japanese Grammar

1. Structure of Japanese

A Japanese sentence basically comprises a predicate and other elements.

predicate

李さんは
Ri-san wa

日本語を
Nihon-go o

使います (use)
tsukaimasu

Ms. Li uses Japanese.

2. Predicate

The predicate is the most important element in a sentence.

(1) The position of a predicate

In Japanese, a predicate comes at the end of a sentence as in the example given below.

李さんは
Ri-san wa

日本語を
Nihon-go o

使います (use)
tsukaimasu

subject

object

predicate

The typical construction of a sentence in Japanese is thus subject + object + predicate.

(2) Types of predicates

In Japanese, verbs, adjectives, and nouns + desu are used as predicates. Depending on inflection, the adjectives are divided into two groups: i-adjectives and na-adjectives.

Examples of verbs, i-adjectives, na-adjectives and nouns are given below.

verb: 　　　使います tsukaimasu (use)　行きます ikimasu (go)
　　　　　　読みます yomimasu (read)　食べます tabemasu (eat)

i-adjective: 　おもしろい omoshiroi (interesting)　暑い atsui (hot)
　　　　　　寒い samui (cold)

na-adjective: 便利 [な] benri[na] (convenient)　元気 [な] genki[na] (healthy)
　　　　　　静か [な] shizuka[na] (quiet)

noun: 　　　わたし watashi (I)　本 hon (book)　かばん kaban (bag)
　　　　　　日本語 Nihon-go (Japanese)

Below are examples where these are used as predicates.

verb: 　　　李さんは日本語を使います。
　　　　　　Ri-san wa Nihon-go o tsukaimasu.
　　　　　　Ms. Li uses Japanese.

i-adjective:	『はじめのいっぽ』はおもしろいです。
	"Hajime no Ippo" wa omoshiroi desu.
	Hajime no Ippo is interesting.
na-adjective:	『はじめのいっぽ』は便利です。
	"Hajime no Ippo" wa benri desu.
	Hajime no Ippo is handy.
noun＋desu:	李さんは中国人です。
	Ri-san wa Chuugoku-jin desu.
	Ms. Li is a Chinese.

3. Verbs

Verbs in Japanese perform a grammatical role through conjugation.

(1) Verbs are divided into one of three groups according to the way they conjugate.

Group Ⅰ verbs:

The vowel immediately before masu is pronounced i.

Examples: 行きます ikimasu (go)　読みます yomimasu (read)
　　　　　話します hanashimasu (talk)　知ります shirimasu (know)

Group Ⅱ verbs:

The vowel immediately before masu is pronounced e.

Examples: 食べます tabemasu (eat)　出ます demasu (go out)
　　　　　開けます akemasu (open)

However, this group of verbs contains some exceptions, and in these the vowel before masu has the sound of i.

Examples: 見ます mimasu (see)　起きます okimasu (get up)

Group Ⅲ verbs:

There are only two verbs that belong to this group. They are characterized by irregular conjugation.

Examples: します shimasu (do)　来ます kimasu (come)

(2) Forms

Verbs change their forms to perform a grammatical role. There are several different forms.

1. Masu-form: iki[masu], tabe[masu]
2. Te-form: itte, tabete (See **Grammatical Notes 2**, p. 137.)
3. Nai-form: ika[nai], tabe[nai] (See **Grammatical Notes 1**, p. 163.)
4. Dictionary form: iku, taberu (See **Grammatical Notes 4**, p. 125.)
5. Ta-form: itta, tabeta (See **Grammatical Notes 3**, p. 156.)

(3) Following phrases

Verbs have different meanings depending on the combinations of the above-mentioned forms and certain following phrases.

Example: te-form + kudasai = request

行ってください。Itte kudasai.　Please go.

食べてください。Tabete kudasai.　Please eat.

Example: ta-form + koto ga arimasu = experience

行ったことがあります。Itta koto ga arimasu.

[I] have been there before.

食べたことがあります。Tabeta koto ga arimasu.

[I] have eaten it before.

4. Adverbs

The following are examples of Japanese adverbs.

時々 tokidoki (sometimes)　少し sukoshi (a little)　ゆっくり yukkuri (slowly)

5. Particles

If in Japanese a sentence is constructed by combining only the aforesaid parts of speech, the result will be:

李さん　日本語　使います。

Ri-san Nihon-go tsukaimasu.

Such a sentence is far from being perfect. What, then, are the differences between this sentence and the one on page 25? In the sentence on page 25, Ri-san is followed by wa, and Nihon-go by o. Such parts of speech as wa and o are called particles, which are broken down into several groups. This section deals with the frequently used structure particles wa and mo and sentence-final particles.

(1) Structure particles

A structure particle, which is combined with a noun, is used to relate the noun to a predicate. Typical examples of such structure particles are subjective ga and objective o. By inserting properly ga and o in Neko nezumi tabemasu, a complete sentence is made.

猫がねずみを食べます。　Neko ga nezumi o tabemasu.　A cat eats a mouse.

ねずみを猫が食べます。　Nezumi o neko ga tabemasu.　A cat eats a mouse.

| 猫をねずみが食べます。 | Neko o nezumi ga tabemasu. | A mouse eats a cat. |
| ねずみが猫を食べます。 | Nezumi ga neko o tabemasu. | A mouse eats a cat. |

As these examples show, the meaning of a sentence is reversed by using different particles, even when the sequence of words remains the same. In other words, the meaning of a sentence is not affected by a change in the sequence of words, as long as the same particles are used.

(2) wa and mo

Both wa and mo are particles that indicate the topic of a sentence.

わたしは日本語を使います。

Watashi wa Nihon-go o tsukaimasu.

I use Japanese.

In this sentence, watashi is the topic.

『はじめのいっぽ』はわたしが買いました。

"Hajime no Ippo" wa watashi ga kaimashita.

Hajime no Ippo was bought by me.

"Hajime no Ippo" is the object of the verb kaimashita, but here it is the topic of the sentence. When the particle mo is used, the meaning of 'also' or 'too' is added.

アリさんも日本語を使います。

Ari-san mo Nihon-go o tsukaimasu.

Ali also uses Japanese.

(3) Sentence-final particles

This type of particle is attached to the end of a sentence and is used in the following ways:

a) To express or imply some feeling on the part of the speaker

b) To express prohibition

c) To indicate a question

Ne: Indicates that the speaker is seeking consent or confirmation.

Example: 日本語を使いますね。

Nihon-go o tsukaimasu ne.

You use Japanese, don't you?

28

Yo: Indicates that the speaker is giving information that the listener doesn't know.

Example: 日本語を使いますよ。

       Nihon-go o tsukaimasu yo.

       I do use Japanese.

Na: Indicates that the sentence is prohibitive.

Example: 日本語を使うな。

       Nihon-go o tsukau na.

       Don't use Japanese.

Ka: Indicates that the sentence is interrogative.

Example: 日本語を使いますか。

       Nihon-go o tsukaimasu ka.

       Do you use Japanese?

(4) Ellipsis

When elements normally included in a sentence are self-evident because of the context, they can be omitted.

マリオ：李さんは日本語を使いますか。   Mario: Ri-san wa Nihon-go o
　李　：はい、使います。マリオさんは？   tsukaimasu ka.
マリオ：使いますよ。   Ri: Hai, tsukaimasu. Mario-san wa?
          Mario: Tsukaimasu yo.

Mario: Do you use Japanese, Ms. Li?
Li: Yes, I do. What about you, Mario?
Mario: I do.

In Ms. Li's answer, the words Watashi wa Nihon-go o are omitted before tsukaimasu. Her question Mario-san wa? is not a full interrogative sentence. To make it complete, these words should be followed by Nihon-go o tsukaimasu ka. Mario also answers in an abbreviated form, saying Tsukaimasu yo, instead of Watashi mo Nihon-go o tsukaimasu yo.

1

<ruby>紹介<rt>しょうかい</rt></ruby>する　Shookai-suru

Introducing Yourself

👀 Dialogues

Ⅰ. At a party/Asking someone's name

マリオ：こんにちは。はじめまして。
高橋：あ、こんにちは。
マリオ：わたしはマリオです。どうぞ
　　　　よろしく。
高橋：は？
マリオ：<u>マ・リ・オです。</u>
　　　　str. 4-1, p. 107
高橋：マリオさん。
マリオ：そうです。あのう、お名前
　　　　は？
高橋：わたしは高橋です。
マリオ：た・か？
高橋：た・か・は・し。*(Giving Mario a*
　　　　business card) どうぞ。
マリオ：あ、どうも。<u>高橋</u>さんですね。
　　　　str. 2-1, p. 107
高橋：ええ、よろしく。

Mario:　　Konnichiwa.
　　　　　Hajimemashite.
Takahashi: A, konnichiwa.
Mario:　　Watashi wa Mario desu.
　　　　　Doozo yoroshiku.
Takahashi: Ha?
Mario:　　<u>Ma-ri-o desu.</u>
　　　　　str. 4-1, p. 107
Takahashi: Mario-san.
Mario:　　Soo desu.　Anoo, o-namae
　　　　　wa?
Takahashi: Watashi wa Takahashi desu.
Mario:　　Ta-ka?
Takahashi: Ta-ka-ha-shi.　*(Giving Mario a*
　　　　　business card) Doozo.
Mario:　　A, doomo. <u>Takahashi-san</u>
　　　　　str. 2-1, p. 107
　　　　　desu ne.
Takahashi: Ee, yoroshiku.

32

Mario:　　Hello. How do you do?
Takahashi: Oh. How do you do?
Mario:　　My name is Mario. Nice to meet
　　　　　you.
Takahashi: Pardon me?
Mario:　　Ma-ri-o.
Takahashi: Mario.
Mario:　　Yes. Er-r-r, may I have your
　　　　　name?
Takahashi: I'm Takahashi.
Mario:　　Ta-ka...?
Takahashi: Ta-ka-ha-shi. *(Giving Mario a*
　　　　　business card) Here you are.
Mario:　　Oh, thank you. So you are Ms.
　　　　　Takahashi.
Takahashi: Yes. Pleased to meet you.

こんにちは。Konnichiwa. Hello. はじめまして。Hajimemashite. How do you do? わたし watashi I どう
ぞよろしく。Doozo yoroshiku. Pleased to meet you. は？ Ha? Pardon me?/Sorry? ～さん ～-san Mr./Ms. ～
そうです。Soo desu. Yes./That's right. あのう anoo Well.../Er..r.. （お）名前 (o-)namae name どうぞ。
Doozo. Here you are./Please. あ a oh どうも。Doomo. Thank you. ええ ee yes

Ⅱ. Asking someone's nationality

高橋：マリオさん、お国は？
マリオ：おくに？おくに…何ですか。
　　　　str. 1-5, p. 106
高橋：あのう、お国はアメリカです
　　　　か。ペルーですか。
マリオ：ああ、ブラジルです。
高橋：そうですか。ブラジルのどこで
　　　　すか。…リオデジャネイロ？
マリオ：いいえ、サンパウロです。
高橋：ああ、サンパウロですか。

Takahashi: Mario-san, o-kuni wa?
Mario:　　O-kuni? O-kuni… <u>Nan</u>
　　　　　　str. 1-5, p. 106
　　　　　　<u>desu ka</u>.
Takahashi: Anoo, o-kuni wa Amerika
　　　　　　desu ka. Peruu desu ka.
Mario:　　Aa, Burajiru desu.
Takahashi: Soo desu ka. Burajiru no
　　　　　　doko desu ka. …Riode-
　　　　　　janeiro?
Mario:　　Iie, Sanpauro desu.
Takahashi: Aa, Sanpauro desu ka.

Takahashi: Mario-san, what is your 'o-kuni'
　　　　　　(where are you from)?
Mario:　　'O-kuni'? 'O-kuni'... What is
　　　　　　that?
Takahashi: Well, is your home country the
　　　　　　United States or Peru?
Mario:　　Oh, it's Brazil.
Takahashi: I see. Which part of Brazil? Rio
　　　　　　de Janeiro?
Mario:　　No, I'm from Sao Paulo.
Takahashi: Oh, Sao Paulo. I see.

ブラジル
Burajiru

（お）国 (o-)kuni home country　何ですか。Nan desu ka. What is it?　アメリカ Amerika America　ペルー
Peruu Peru　ああ aa oh　ブラジル Burajiru Brazil　そうですか。Soo desu ka. I see.　どこ doko where/which
part　リオデジャネイロ Riodejaneiro Rio de Janeiro　いいえ iie no　サンパウロ Sanpauro Sao Paulo

Ⅲ. Asking someone's job

高橋：お仕事は？
マリオ：仕事は… construction.
高橋：ああ、建築ですね。
マリオ：け・ん・ち・く。建築です。
str. 4-1, p. 107

Takahashi: O-shigoto wa?
Mario: Shigoto wa… 'construction'.
Takahashi: Aa, kenchiku desu ne.
Mario: <u>Ke-n-chi-ku</u>. Kenchiku
str. 4-1, p. 107
desu.

Takahashi: What do you do?
Mario: I'm in...construction.
Takahashi: Oh, you do 'kenchiku,' don't you?
Mario: 'Ke-n-chi-ku.' Yes, 'kenchiku.'

(お)仕事 (o-)shigoto job/occupation 建築 kenchiku construction/building

Grammatical Notes

1. ～は～です。 ～ wa ～ desu. (Basic structure of a noun sentence)

The particle wa indicates that the preceding word is the topic of the sentence. A sentence ending with desu is in the polite style.

| わたしはマリオです。 | Watashi wa Mario desu. | I'm Mario. |
| 国はブラジルです。 | Kuni wa Burajiru desu. | My home country is Brazil. |

2. ～か。 ～ ka. (Basic structure of an interrogative sentence)

A sentence ending with ka is an interrogative one. There is a rise in pitch on the final syllable.

あなたはマリオさんですか。	Anata wa Mario-san desu ka.	Are you Mario?
お国はブラジルですか。	O-kuni wa Burajiru desu ka.	Is your home country Brazil?
何ですか。	Nan desu ka.	What is it?

3. はい（ええ）、～です。 Hai (Ee), ～ desu. (Affirmative sentences)

The following are affirmative answers to questions.

マリオさんですか。	Mario-san desu ka.	Are you Mario?
はい、マリオです。	Hai, Mario desu.	Yes, I'm Mario.
お国はアメリカですか。	O-kuni wa Amerika desu ka.	Is your home country the United States?
はい、アメリカです。	Hai, Amerika desu.	Yes, it is the United States.

4. いいえ、～では（じゃ）ありません。 Iie, ～ dewa (ja) arimasen. (Negative sentences)

The following are negative answers to questions.

マリオさんですか。	Mario-san desu ka.	Are you Mario?
いいえ、マリオではありません。	Iie, Mario dewa arimasen.	No, I'm not Mario.
お国はペルーですか。	O-kuni wa Peruu desu ka.	Is your home country Peru?
いいえ、ペルーではありません。	Iie, Peruu dewa arimasen.	No, it is not Peru.

5. ～さん ～-san (Using family names)

The suffix san is used regardless of sex or marital status. It is customary for Japanese people to call each other by their family names.

| ♀高橋かおり＝高橋さん | Takahashi Kaori=Takahashi-san | Ms. Takahashi |
| ♂田中一郎　＝田中さん | Tanaka Ichiroo =Tanaka-san | Mr. Tanaka |

35

あなた anata you

6. 〜は？ 〜 wa ? (Asking questions)

When it is self-evident from the context what question the speaker is going to ask, the sentence ends in an incomplete way and with a rising intonation. This sounds more natural.

お名前は何ですか。

O-namae wa nan desu ka. → O-namae wa?

What is your name?

お名前は？

Your name?

お仕事は何ですか。

O-shigoto wa nan desu ka. → O-shigoto wa?

What is your occupation?

お仕事は？

Your occupation?

お国はどこですか。

O-kuni wa doko desu ka. → O-kuni wa?

What is your home country?

お国は？

Your home country?

7. 〜の〜 〜 no 〜 (Noun modifier)

The particle no connects nouns to give a variety of meanings. In the context of the above conversation, no is used to specify a smaller part (city) of a much larger area (country).

| ブラジルのサンパウロ | Burajiru no Sanpauro | Sao Paulo in Brazil |
| アメリカのニューヨーク | Amerika no Nyuuyooku | New York in the U.S. |

ニューヨーク Nyuuyooku New York

 **Exercises**

1. Substitution drill: Introducing yourself

高橋：こんにちは。わたしは高橋です。
　　　あのう、お名前は？
　A：はじめまして。（マリオ）です。
　　　どうぞよろしく。

Takahashi: Konnichiwa. Watashi wa Takahashi desu. Anoo, o-namae wa?
A: Hajimemashite. (Mario) desu. Doozo yoroshiku.

例 Ree：マリオ Mario　① アリ Ari　② あなたの名前 anata no namae

2. When you cannot catch some word or phrase, do the following.

A：お名前は？　　　　　　A: O-namae wa?
B：（高橋）です。　　　　B: (Takahashi) desu.
A：（たか）？　　　　　　A: (Taka)?
B：（た・か・は・し）です。　B: (Ta-ka-ha-shi) desu.
A：（高橋）さん。　　　　A: (Takahashi)-san.

例 Ree：高橋 Takahashi　① 中林 Nakabayashi　② 渡辺 Watanabe

3. Write your own business card in katakana (see "Fukubukuro").

Practice the following dialogue and try introducing yourself to a Japanese using the business card.

①はじめまして。
　わたしは（　　　　）です。
　あのう、お名前は？
Hajimemashite.
Watashi wa (　　　) desu.
Anoo, o-namae wa?

②高橋です。
Takahashi desu.

③高橋さんですね。
　どうぞよろしく。
Takahashi-san desu ne.
Doozo yoroshiku.

高　橋
Takahashi

例 ree example

4. Substitution drill: Asking the meaning of words

A：あのう、（お国）は？   A: Anoo, (o-kuni) wa?
B：（おくに）？ 何ですか？   B: (O-kuni)? Nan desu ka.

例 Ree：お国 o-kuni   ① お仕事 o-shigoto   ② お住まい o-sumai

5. Substitution drill: Answering questions

A：お名前は？   A: O-namae wa?
B：（李）です。   B: (Ri) desu.
A：お仕事は？   A: O-shigoto wa?
B：（プログラマー）です。   B: (Puroguramaa) desu.
A：お国は？   A: O-kuni wa?
B：（中国）です。   B: (Chuugoku) desu.

例 Ree：李さん Ri-san, プログラマー puroguramaa, 中国 Chuugoku
① ナンシーさん Nanshii-san, 銀行員 ginkooin, オーストラリア Oosutoraria
② あなた anata, あなたの仕事 anata no shigoto, あなたの国 anata no kuni

6. Substitution drill: Asking questions

A：あのう、お国は？   A: Anoo, o-kuni wa?
B：（ブラジル）です。   B: (Burajiru) desu.
A：（ブラジル）のどこですか。   A: (Burajiru) no doko desu ka.
B：（サンパウロ）です。   B: (Sanpauro) desu.

例 Ree：ブラジル Burajiru, サンパウロ Sanpauro
① イラン Iran, テヘラン Teheran
② あなたの国 anata no kuni, あなたの町 anata no machi

38

お住まい o-sumai (one's) house　プログラマー puroguramaa programmer　中国 Chuugoku China　銀行員
ginkooin bank employee　オーストラリア Oosutoraria Australia　イラン Iran Iran　テヘラン Teheran Tehran

 # Fukubukuro

1. Writing your name in Japanese

Learn to write your name in katakana using the katakana table on pages 20-21. (Ask a Japanese how to write the letters.)

Mario	Bambang
マリオ	バンバン

Tanom	Ferguson
タノム	ファーガソン

Connect corresponding names with a line.

(1)クリントン・   ・a. Steve
(2)エリザベス・   ・b. Gandhi
(3)スティーブ・   ・c. Elizabeth
(4)スカルノ　・   ・d. Clinton
(5)ガンジー　・   ・e. Sukarno

2. Useful words

a. お仕事は？ **O-shigoto wa?** (What is) your occupation?

教師	kyooshi	teacher
学生	gakusee	student
エンジニア	enjinia	engineer
主婦	shufu	housewife

> Ask a Japanese colleague how to say your profession/occupation in Japanese.
> この仕事は日本語で何ですか。
> Kono shigoto wa Nihon-go de nan desu ka.
> How do you say this occupation in Japanese?

b. お国は？ **O-kuni wa?** (What is) your home country?

タイ	Tai	Thailand
マレーシア	Mareeshia	Malaysia
中国	Chuugoku	China
韓国	Kankoku	South Korea

> Ask a Japanese what your country is called in Japanese.
> わたしの国は日本語で何ですか。
> Watashi no kuni wa Nihon-go de nan desu ka.
> What do you call my country in Japanese?

3. What would you do if...?

Have you ever noticed differences in customs between your country and Japan while talking with a Japanese?

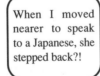

In my country, people look into each other's eyes when speaking, but...

When I moved nearer to speak to a Japanese, she stepped back?!!

In greeting, people kiss or hug each other in my country.

And you?

Good morning.

Good afternoon.
(This is not normally said to one's colleagues or family.)

Good evening.

Goodbye.

Mr. A: Are you fine?
Ms. B: Yes.

Note: Without the words in brackets, the expressions are much more informal in style.

Mr. A: <Lit. I'm going before you.>
Mr. B: <Lit. You must be very tired.>

Good night.

Mr. A: Please.
Mr. B: Thank you.

Doozo: An expression widely used to encourage someone to eat, accept, or do something.

Doomo: Besides 'thank you,' it has, depending on the circumstances and who you are talking to, such meanings as 'sorry' and 'excuse me.'

Ms. A: Thank you.
Mr. B: My pleasure.

Mr. A: I'm sorry. Excuse me.
Mr. B: That's all right.

42

<Set phrase used before eating or drinking>   <Set phrase used after eating or drinking>

<F>: formal expressions
<Inf>: informal expressions

Mr. A: Congratulations.
Mr. & Ms. B: Thank you.

Mr. A: Excuse me.
Mr. B: Come in.

Mr. A: See you later.
Ms. A: Be back soon.
(When leaving your home or office, to where you will certainly return, you say, '<Inf>Itte kimasu' ('<F>Itte mairimasu').)

Mr. A: I'm back.
Ms. A: Welcome back.
(When you return to your home or office, you say, 'Tadaima.')

2

買う　Kau

Shopping

👀 Dialogues

I. At a supermarket/Asking where to find something

リ　サ：	<u>あのう、すみません。</u>
	str. 5-1, p.107
	せっけんはどこですか。
店　員：	ええと、あそこです。
リ　サ：	<u>あそこ？</u>
	str. 2-1, p.107
店　員：	ええ。レジの前です。
リ　サ：	<u>レジの前ですね。</u> <u>どうも。</u>
	str. 2-1, p.107　　*str. 5-2, p.107*

Risa:	<u>Anoo, sumimasen</u>.
	str. 5-1, p.107
	Sekken wa doko desu ka.
Ten'in:	Eeto, asoko desu.
Risa:	<u>Asoko?</u>
	str. 2-1, p.107
Ten'in:	Ee. Reji no mae desu.
Risa:	<u>Reji no mae desu ne</u>. <u>Doomo</u>.
	str. 2-1, p.107　　*str. 5-2, p.107*

Lisa:　Excuse me. Where can I find soap?

Clerk:　Well, it's over there.

Lisa:　Over there?

Clerk:　Yes. In front of the checkout counter.

Lisa:　In front of the checkout counter. Thank you.

すみません。 Sumimasen. Excuse me.　せっけん sekken soap　どこ doko where　あそこ asoko (over) there
レジ reji checkout counter/cash register　前 mae (in) front (of)　どうも。 Doomo. Thanks.

II. At a kiosk/Asking the price

ア　リ：これ、ください。
店　員：はい。
ア　リ：いくらですか。
店　員：220円です。
ア　リ：はい。*(He pays.)* どうも。

Ari:　　Kore, kudasai.
Ten'in: Hai.
Ari:　　Ikura desu ka.
Ten'in: 220-en desu.
Ari:　　Hai. *(He pays.)* Doomo.

Ali:　　I would like to buy this.
Clerk: O.K.
Ali:　　How much is it?
Clerk: 220 yen.
Ali:　　Here you are. *(He pays.)* Thank you.

III. At the front desk of a hotel/Asking if something is available

[Available]
ロバート：　あのう、テレホンカード、
　　　　　　ありますか。
ホテルの人：はい。こちらです。
ロバート：　じゃ、それ、ください。

Robaato:　　Anoo, terehon-kaado,
　　　　　　arimasu ka.
Hoteru no hito: Hai.　Kochira desu.
Robaato:　　Ja, sore, kudasai.

47

Robert:　　Are telephone cards available
　　　　　　here?
Receptionist: Sure. Here they are.
Robert:　　O.K., I'll take this.

[Not available]
ロバート：　あのう、テレホンカード、
　　　　　　ありますか。
ホテルの人：テレホンカードはちょっと。
ロバート：　そうですか。どうも。

Robaato:　　Anoo, terehon-kaado,
　　　　　　arimasu ka.
Hoteru no hito: Terehon-kaado wa chotto.
Robaato:　　Soo desu ka.　Doomo.

Robert:　　Are telephone cards available
　　　　　　here?
Receptionist: No, I'm afraid not.
Robert:　　Oh, well, thank you.

これ **kore** this　ください **kudasai** <lit. please give me>　いくら **ikura** how much　テレホンカード **terehon-kaado** telephone card　こちら **kochira** here/this way/this side　それ **sore** it/that　ちょっと **chotto** <lit. a little>
そうですか。 **Soo desu ka.** I see.

 **Grammatical Notes**

1. ～は ここ/そこ/あそこ です。 **～ wa koko/soko/asoko desu.**
   (Indicating something's position)
   These expressions are used to indicate a location relative to the positions of the speaker and the listener.

ここ koko = near the speaker   そこ soko = near the listener

あそこ asoko = far from both the speaker and the listener

When you want to ask where something is, you can use the following expression:
   ～はどこですか。   ～ wa doko desu ka.   Where can I find ～ ?

Examples:

A：かばんはどこですか。	Kaban wa doko desu ka.	Where can I find bags?
B：かばんはここです。	Kaban wa koko desu.	Bags are here.
A：魚はどこですか。	Sakana wa doko desu ka.	Where can I find fish?
B：魚はそこです。	Sakana wa soko desu.	Fish are there.
A：ペンはどこですか。	Pen wa doko desu ka.	Where can I find pens?
B：ペンはあそこです。	Pen wa asoko desu.	Pens are over there.

cf.) The following expressions are used to indicate an object by means of its relative position to the speaker and the listener:
   これ kore = this (near the speaker)
   それ sore = that (near the listener)
   あれ are = that (far from the speaker and the listener)

かばん kaban bag 魚 sakana fish ペン pen pen

2. ～は～の前/後ろ/近く です。 ～ wa ～ no mae/ushiro/chikaku desu.
(Indicating something's position)

These expressions are used to indicate the position of something relative to another thing.

Examples:

レジの前です。	Reji no mae desu.	(It is) in front of the cash register.
果物の後ろです。	Kudamono no ushiro desu.	(It is) behind the fruit.
入り口の近くです。	Iriguchi no chikaku desu.	(It is) near the entrance.

 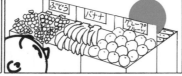 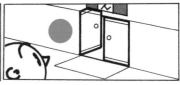

3. ～（を）ください。 ～ (o) kudasai. (Please give me ～.)

This expression (which literally means 'give me ～') is used when you have decided to buy something.

4. ～は ありますか。 ～ wa arimasu ka. (Do you have ～ ?)

This is an expression for asking if something that you are looking for is available in a store, just as in the following dialogues between a customer and a clerk.

Examples:

A：たばこはありますか。	Tabako wa arimasu ka.	Do you sell cigarettes here?
B：はい。	Hai.	Yes, we do.
A：かみそりはありますか。	Kamisori wa arimasu ka.	Do you sell razors here?
B：かみそりはちょっと。	Kamisori wa chotto.	I'm afraid not.

5. いくらですか。 Ikura desu ka. (How much is/are ～ ?)

This is a typical way of asking the price of something.

Examples:

A：これ、いくらですか。	Kore, ikura desu ka.	How much is this?
B：200円です。	200-en desu.	It is 200 yen.
A：ティッシュ、いくらですか。	Tisshu, ikura desu ka.	How much are the tissues?
B：160円です。	160-en desu.	They're 160 yen.

49

後ろ ushiro behind/back　近く chikaku near/close　果物 kudamono fruit　入り口 iriguchi entrance　たばこ tabako cigarette　かみそり kamisori razor　ティッシュ tisshu tissue

 **Exercises**

1. Match the pictures with the words.

(1) ここです。　　　Koko desu.(　)
(2) そこです。　　　Soko desu.(　)
(3) あそこです。　　Asoko desu.(　)
(4) 入り口の近くです。Iriguchi no chikaku desu.(　)
(5) レジの前です。　Reji no mae desu.(　)

2. Now you are going shopping to buy the things listed in the box.

Shopping list:
例 Ree：洗剤 senzai　① 歯ブラシ haburashi　② タオル taoru　③ 果物 kudamono

(1) Referring to the picture of the shop below, ask the location of the items listed.

あなた：あのう、すみません。　　　　Anata: Anoo, sumimasen.
　　　　（洗剤）はどこですか。　　　　　　　　（Senzai) wa doko desu ka.
店　員：（レジの前）です。　　　　Ten'in: (Reji no mae) desu.
あなた：（レジの前）ですね。どうも。Anata: (Reji no mae) desu ne. Doomo.

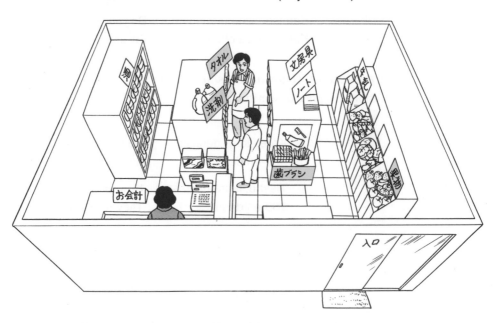

洗剤 senzai detergent　歯ブラシ haburashi toothbrush　タオル taoru towel

(2) Substitution drill: Ask the availability of the items listed on the previous page.

> あなた：あのう、（洗剤）、ありますか。
> Anata: Anoo, (senzai), arimasu ka.

> 店　員：はい、こちらです。
> あなた：じゃ、それ、ください。
> Ten'in: Hai, kochira desu.
> Anata: Ja, sore, kudasai.

> 店　員：（洗剤）はちょっと。
> あなた：そうですか。どうも。
> Ten'in: (Senzai) wa chotto.
> Anata: Soo desu ka. Doomo.

3. **Make a shopping list of your own to do real shopping. If there are any words that you do not know, look them up in a dictionary or ask a Japanese.**

 **Fukubukuro**

1. Bargain sales

1.1 Here are some bills for bargain sales. Identify the words and the pictures that correspond to each other.

(1) Big Thank-You Sale (　) (2) 30% Off (　) (3) Sale (　) (4) Half Price (　)
(5) Very Cheap (　) (6) Bargains (　)

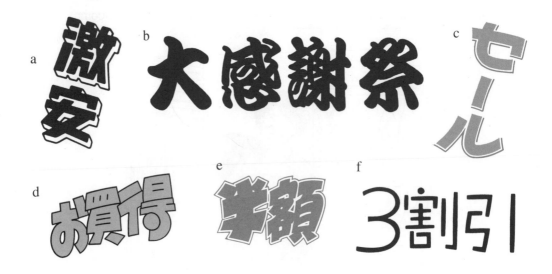

1.2 Write the Chinese character meaning 'off.'

2. What would you do if...?

When you buy something at a kiosk or a small retail shop with no cash register, you have to ask the Japanese person at the shop the price. What would you do if you were not sure that you could hear or understand the price the person would tell you?

I would shop only at a supermarket or a convenience store.

I would show all the money that I had and ask the person to take as much as necessary.

I would take a note pad and ask him to write the price.

And you?

お買得 okaidoku bargain　激安 gekiyasu very cheap　大感謝祭 dai-kanshasai big thank-you sale　3割引き 3-waribiki 30% off　セール seeru bargain sale　半額 hangaku half price

1. Numerals

0	ゼロ	zero							
	れい	ree							
1	いち	ichi	11	じゅういち	juu ichi	30	さんじゅう	san-juu	
2	に	ni	12	じゅうに	juu ni	40	よんじゅう	yon-juu	
3	さん	san	13	じゅうさん	juu san	50	ごじゅう	go-juu	
4	よん	yon	14	じゅうよん	juu yon	60	ろくじゅう	roku-juu	
	し	shi		じゅうし	juu shi	70	ななじゅう	nana-juu	
5	ご	go	15	じゅうご	juu go		しちじゅう	shichi-juu	
6	ろく	roku	16	じゅうろく	juu roku	80	はちじゅう	hachi-juu	
7	なな	nana	17	じゅうなな	juu nana	90	きゅうじゅう	kyuu-juu	
	しち	shichi		じゅうしち	juu shichi				
8	はち	hachi	18	じゅうはち	juu hachi				
9	きゅう	kyuu	19	じゅうきゅう	juu kyuu				
	く	ku		じゅうく	juu ku				
10	じゅう	juu	20	にじゅう	ni-juu				

100	ひゃく	hyaku	1,000	せん	sen
200	にひゃく	ni-hyaku	2,000	にせん	ni-sen
300	さんびゃく	san-byaku	3,000	さんぜん	san-zen
400	よんひゃく	yon-hyaku	4,000	よんせん	yon-sen
500	ごひゃく	go-hyaku	5,000	ごせん	go-sen
600	ろっぴゃく	rop-pyaku	6,000	ろくせん	roku-sen
700	ななひゃく	nana-hyaku	7,000	ななせん	nana-sen
800	はっぴゃく	hap-pyaku	8,000	はっせん	has-sen
900	きゅうひゃく	kyuu-hyaku	9,000	きゅうせん	kyuu-sen
10,000	いちまん	ichi-man	100,000	じゅうまん	juu-man

2. Do you know how to pronounce the following numbers?

9	きゅう	kyuu
23	にじゅうさん	ni-juu san
416	よんひゃくじゅうろく	yon-hyaku juu roku
7,890	ななせんはっぴゃくきゅうじゅう	nana-sen hap-pyaku kyuu-juu
72,341	ななまんにせんさんびゃくよんじゅういち	nana-man ni-sen san-byaku yon-juu ichi
618,905	ろくじゅういちまんはっせんきゅうひゃくご	roku-juu ichi-man has-sen kyuu-hyaku go

3. How to say telephone numbers

Like in English, each figure should be given separately. The hyphen between figures is read no.

0	3	—	3	2	9	2	—	6	1	9	1
ゼロ	さん	の	さん	に	きゅう	に	の	ろく	いち	きゅう	いち
zero	san	no	san	ni	kyuu	ni	no	roku	ichi	kyuu	ichi

3
食べる　Taberu
Eating

👀 Dialogues

Ⅰ. At a restaurant/Attracting attention

ア リ：<u>すみません</u>。
str. 5-1, p. 107
店 員：はい。お待たせしました。

Ari:	<u>Sumimasen</u>.
	str. 5-1, p. 107
Ten'in:	Hai. O-matase shimashita.

Ali: Excuse me.
Waitress: Yes, sir. Sorry to have kept you waiting.

Ⅱ. Ordering

ア リ：エビグラタンとサラダ。
店 員：はい。
李 ：*(Pointing to the menu)* これは何です
　　　　か。
店 員：ビーフカレーです。
李 ：じゃ、これ、お願いします。
店 員：お飲み物はよろしいですか。
ア リ：<u>ええと</u>、コーヒー。
str. 3-1, p. 107
李 ：コーヒー２つ、お願いします。
店 員：以上でよろしいですか。
ア リ：はい。

Ari:	Ebi-guratan to sarada.
Ten'in:	Hai.
Ri:	*(Pointing to the menu)* Kore wa nan desu ka.
Ten'in:	Biifu-karee desu.
Ri:	Ja, kore, onegai-shimasu.
Ten'in:	O-nomimono wa yoroshii desu ka.
Ari:	<u>Eeto</u>, koohii.
	str. 3-1, p. 107
Ri:	Koohii futatsu, onegai-shimasu.
Ten'in:	Ijoo de yoroshii desu ka.
Ari:	Hai.

Ali: A shrimp gratin and a salad.
Waitress: Right.
Li: *(Pointing to the menu)* What is this?
Waitress: It's beef curry.
Li: O.K., I'll have this.
Waitress: Something to drink?
Ali: Well, I'll have coffee.
Li: Two coffees, please.
Waitress: Is that all?
Ali: Yes.

56

待たせます matasemasu keep someone waiting エビ ebi shrimp グラタン guratan gratin と to and サラダ
sarada salad これ kore this 何 nan what ビーフカレー biifu-karee beef curry じゃ ja so 飲み物
nomimono beverage/drink よろしい yoroshii O.K./all right コーヒー koohii coffee ２つ futatsu two

III. Asking about one's order

アリ：<u>すみません</u>。
str. 5-1, p. 107
店員：はい。
アリ：あのう、エビグラタン、まだ
　　　ですか。
店員：あ、申し訳ありません。すぐ
　　　できます。

Ari:　　Sumimasen.
str. 5-1, p. 107
Ten'in: Hai.
Ari:　　Anoo, ebi-guratan, mada desu
　　　　ka.
Ten'in: A, mooshiwake arimasen. Sugu
　　　　dekimasu.

Ali:　　　Excuse me.
Waitress: Yes.
Ali:　　　Er. Is the shrimp gratin not ready
　　　　　yet?
Waitress: Oh, I'm sorry. It will be served
　　　　　shortly.

57

まだ mada (not) yet 申し訳ありません。Mooshiwake arimasen. I'm sorry. すぐ sugu soon できます dekimasu will be ready/served

Grammatical Notes

1. これ／それ／あれは〜です。**Kore/Sore/Are wa 〜 desu. (Saying what something is)**

This expression is used to identify something. Depending on the relative positions of the speaker, the listener and the thing being referred to, a choice is made from among 'this (kore),' 'that (sore)' and 'that (are).' (See **Grammatical Notes 1**, p. 48.)

An interrogative sentence using one of these is as follows:

これ／それ／あれは何ですか。 Kore/Sore/Are wa nan desu ka.

What is this/that/that?

Examples:

ナンシー：これは何ですか。　Nanshii: Kore wa nan desu ka.
店　員：コロッケです。　　 Ten'in:　Korokke desu.
Nancy:　　What is this?
Waitress: (It's) a croquette.

ナンシー：それは何ですか。　Nanshii: Sore wa nan desu ka.
店　員：卵です。　　　　　 Ten'in:　Tamago desu.
Nancy:　　What is that?
Clerk:　　(This is) an egg.

ナンシー：あれは何ですか。　Nanshii: Are wa nan desu ka.
店　員：ビーフシチューです。 Ten'in:　Biifu-shichuu desu.
Nancy:　　What is that?
Waitress: (That's) beef stew.

2. 1つ、2つ、3つ… **hitotsu, futatsu, mittsu… (Counting things)**

This way of counting can be used for various things. The pictures below show the Japanese way of counting things using fingers.

ひとつ hitotsu　　ふたつ futatsu　　みっつ mittsu　　よっつ yottsu　　いつつ itsutsu

むっつ muttsu　　ななつ nanatsu　　やっつ yattsu　　ここのつ kokonotsu　　とお too

コロッケ korokke croquette　卵 tamago egg　シチュー shichuu stew

58

Examples:

コーヒー3つ　koohii mittsu　three coffees
卵6つ　tamago muttsu　six eggs

When you would like to know how many, say the following:
いくつですか。Ikutsu desu ka. How many?

3. ～、お願いします。 ～, onegai-shimasu. (～, please.)

This expression is used when you are giving an order, buying something, or asking a favor of someone.

When food or a beverage is ordered, the following expressions can be used.

これ、お願いします。
Kore, onegai-shimasu.
This one, please.

チャーシューメン2つ、お願いします。
Chaashuumen futatsu, onegai-shimasu.
Two 'chashumens,' please.

ざるそば1つと、かけそば3つ、お願いします。
Zarusoba hitotsu to, kakesoba mittsu, onegai-shimasu.
One 'zarusoba' and three 'kakesobas,' please.

In the last expression, the particle to, which means 'and,' is used when more than one thing is ordered.

When you would like to order or pay for food or a beverage at a restaurant, say the following:

注文、お願いします。	Chuumon, onegai-shimasu.	Will you take my order, please?
メニュー、お願いします。	Menyuu, onegai-shimasu.	Can I see a menu?
お水、お願いします。	O-mizu, onegai-shimasu.	Water, please.
お勘定、お願いします。	O-kanjoo, onegai-shimasu.	Bill, please.

4. ～、まだですか。 ～, mada desu ka. (～ not ready yet?)

This is a way of hurrying up a waiter when food or a beverage is slow in coming.

In order to attract the waiter's attention, say the following:
すみません。Sumimasen. Excuse me.

You could then say, for example:

ハンバーグ定食、まだですか。
Hanbaagu-teeshoku, mada desu ka.
Is the hamburger set not ready yet?

59

チャーシューメン chaashuumen Chinese noodles with roast pork　ざるそば zarusoba buckwheat noodles　かけそば kakesoba buckwheat noodles in soup　メニュー menyuu menu　（お）水 (o-)mizu water　お勘定 o-kanjoo bill　ハンバーグ hanbaagu hamburger steak　定食 teeshoku a set meal

 **Exercises**

1. Referring to the pictures below, complete the dialogue.

あなた： （これ）は何ですか。   Anata: (Kore) wa nan desu ka.
店　員： （ハムサンド）です。   Ten'in: (Hamu-sando) desu.

例 Ree：   (1)   (2)

2. Substitution drill: Ordering food

A： （ハムサンド）、お願いします。   A: (Hamu-sando), onegai-shimasu.

例 Ree：ハムサンド hamu-sando	￥600
ハンバーガー hanbaagaa	￥450
グラタン guratan	￥750
ミックスサンド mikkusu-sando	￥650
ピラフ pirafu	￥700
ドリア doria	￥750

60

ハム hamu ham サンド sando sandwich ハンバーガー hanbaagaa hamburger ミックス mikkusu mixed
ピラフ pirafu pilaf ドリア doria doria

3. You are now at a restaurant with your family. Referring to the picture, try ordering for them.

あなた：（ハンバーガー１つと
　　　　　ドリア２つ）、お願いします。

店　員：はい。

Anata: (Hanbaagaa hitotsu to doria
　　　　　futatsu), onegai-shimasu.

Ten'in: Hai.

例 Ree : 　　　　　　　　(1)　　　　　　　　　(2)

4. Substitution drill: Hurrying up the waiter (Use the menu on the previous page.)

あなた：すみません。（ハムサンド）、
　　　　　まだですか。

店　員：あ、申し訳ありません。

Anata: Sumimasen. (Hamu-sando),
　　　　　mada desu ka.

Ten'in: A, mooshiwake arimasen.

61

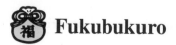
Fukubukuro

1. Useful words

1.1 Identify the corresponding Chinese characters, katakana and English.

例 Ree：野菜　　・
(1) 牛　肉　　・
(2) 豚　肉　　・
(3) 鳥　肉　　・
(4)　魚　　・
(5) 魚貝類　　・

・①ポークpooku　　・
・②チキンchikin　　・
・③フィッシュfisshu　　・
・④シーフードshiifuudo　　・
・⑤ベジタブルbejitaburu　・
・⑥ビーフbiifu　　・

・a. vegetable
・b. seafood
・c. beef
・d. chicken
・e. pork
・f. fish

1.2 What are the following dishes?

(1) (　　　　　)　　　　(2) (　　　　　)　　　　(3) (　　　　　)

① 天丼 tendon　② カツ定食 katsu-teeshoku　③ ラーメン raamen

2. What would you do if... ?

What would you do if you could not read a menu?

I would only eat hamburger steaks.

ハンバーグ、ありますか。
Hanbaagu, arimasu ka.

I would make a note of what I'd eaten so that I could ask for it again.

これ、お願いします。
Kore, onegai-shimasu.

I would order what someone sitting next to me was eating.

あれ、お願いします。
Are, onegai-shimasu.

And you?

天丼 tendon bowl of rice topped with deep-fried prawns　カツ katsu cutlet　ラーメン raamen Chinese noodles

Language Focus **Counting**

1. How to count

In Japanese, there are many different counter suffixes, and the counter suffix you use depends on what you are counting.

	Material things in general		People	
1	ひとつ	hitotsu	ひとり	hitori
2	ふたつ	futatsu	ふたり	futari
3	みっつ	mittsu	さんにん	san-nin
4	よっつ	yottsu	よにん	yo-nin
5	いつつ	itsutsu	ごにん	go-nin
6	むっつ	muttsu	ろくにん	roku-nin
7	ななつ	nanatsu	ななにん	nana-nin
8	やっつ	yattsu	はちにん	hachi-nin
9	ここのつ	kokonotsu	きゅうにん	kyuu-nin
10	とお	too	じゅうにん	juu-nin
?	いくつ	ikutsu	なんにん	nan-nin

	Floors of a building		Years of age	
1	いっかい	ik-kai	いっさい	is-sai
2	にかい	ni-kai	にさい	ni-sai
3	さんがい	san-gai	さんさい	san-sai
4	よんかい	yon-kai	よんさい	yon-sai
5	ごかい	go-kai	ごさい	go-sai
6	ろっかい	rok-kai	ろくさい	roku-sai
7	ななかい	nana-kai	ななさい	nana-sai
8	はっかい	hak-kai	はっさい	has-sai
9	きゅうかい	kyuu-kai	きゅうさい	kyuu-sai
10	じゅっかい	juk-kai	じゅっさい	jus-sai
?	なんがい	nan-gai	なんさい	nan-sai

	Small things		Beverages in a glass or a cup	
1	いっこ	ik-ko	いっぱい	ip-pai
2	にこ	ni-ko	にはい	ni-hai
3	さんこ	san-ko	さんばい	san-bai
4	よんこ	yon-ko	よんはい	yon-hai
5	ごこ	go-ko	ごはい	go-hai
6	ろっこ	rok-ko	ろっぱい	rop-pai
7	ななこ	nana-ko	ななはい	nana-hai
8	はっこ	hak-ko	はっぱい	hap-pai
9	きゅうこ	kyuu-ko	きゅうはい	kyuu-hai
10	じゅっこ	juk-ko	じゅっぱい	jup-pai
?	なんこ	nan-ko	なんばい	nan-bai

2. Prices

The Japanese currency is the yen.

¥1	いちえん	ichi-en
¥10	じゅうえん	juu-en
¥100	ひゃくえん	hyaku-en
¥1,000	せんえん	sen-en
¥10,000	いちまんえん	ichi-man-en
¥?	いくら	ikura

4

話す Hanasu

Talking

👀 Dialogues

Ⅰ. Talking about a wedding photo

ア　リ：	鈴木さん、これ、わたしの妻です。
鈴　木：	へえ、きれいな奥さんですね。結婚式ですか。
ア　リ：	「けっこんしき」？ *str. 1-5, p. 106*
鈴　木：	ええ、結婚式、wedding ceremony。
ア　リ：	ああ、ええ、結婚式です。
鈴　木：	きれいですね。
ア　リ：	あの、鈴木さんは結婚していますか。
鈴　木：	えっ、わたし？…ええ、まあ…
ア　リ：	子どもは？
鈴　木：	ううん…まだ…

(Is Mr. Suzuki avoiding this topic?
See **Fukubukuro**.)

Ari: Suzuki-san, kore, watashi no tsuma desu.

Suzuki: Hee, kireena okusan desu ne. Kekkon-shiki desu ka.

Ari: 'Kekkon-shiki'?
str. 1-5, p. 106

Suzuki: Ee, kekkon-shiki, 'wedding ceremony.'

Ari: Aa, ee, kekkon-shiki desu.

Suzuki: Kiree desu ne.

Ari: Ano, Suzuki-san wa kekkon-shite imasu ka.

Suzuki: E, watashi?…Ee, maa…

Ari: Kodomo wa?

Suzuki: Uun…mada…

(Is Mr. Suzuki avoiding this topic?
See **Fukubukuro**.)

66

Ali: Mr. Suzuki, this is my wife.

Suzuki: Oh, you have a pretty wife. Is this a picture of your 'kekkon-shiki'?

Ali: 'Kekkon-shiki'?

Suzuki: Yes, 'kekkon-shiki' - your wedding ceremony.

Ali: Oh, yes. It's a picture of our wedding ceremony.

Suzuki: It's beautiful.

Ali: Are you married, Mr. Suzuki?

Suzuki: Me? Yes... I...

Ali: Do you have children?

Suzuki: No... Not yet...

妻 tsuma (my) wife　きれい [な] kiree[na] pretty　奥さん okusan (somebody else's) wife　結婚しています
kekkon-shite imasu be married　子ども kodomo children　まだ mada (not) yet

II. Talking about one's family

ロバート：佐藤さん、これ、わたしの
　　　　　家族です。
佐　藤：へえ！これ、奥さん？
ロバート：ええ、そうです。
佐　藤：きれいな奥さんですね…
ロバート：これが、子どもです。
佐　藤：かわいいですね！何歳？
ロバート：10歳、8歳、6歳、4歳。
佐　藤：かわいい…

Robaato: Satoo-san, kore, watashi no
　　　　kazoku desu.
Satoo:　Hee! Kore, okusan?
Robaato: Ee, soo desu.
Satoo:　Kireena okusan desu ne …
Robaato: Kore ga, kodomo desu.
Satoo:　Kawaii desu ne! Nan-sai?
Robaato: 10-sai, 8-sai, 6-sai, 4-sai.
Satoo:　Kawaii…

Robert: Ms. Sato, this is my family.
Sato:　Oh! Is this your wife?
Robert: Yes, it is.
Sato:　Your wife is beautiful!
Robert: These are my children.
Sato:　Very cute! How old are they?
Robert: Ten, eight, six, and four.
Sato:　So cute...

家族 kazoku family　かわいい kawaii cute　何歳 nan-sai how old　〜歳 〜-sai 〜 years old

🗣 Grammatical Notes

1. ～歳 ～-sai (Counter suffix for age)

	0	ゼロさい	zero-sai
	1	いっさい	is-sai
	2	にさい	ni-sai
	3	さんさい	san-sai
	4	よんさい	yon-sai
	5	ごさい	go-sai
	6	ろくさい	roku-sai
	7	ななさい	nana-sai
	8	はっさい	has-sai
	9	きゅうさい	kyuu-sai
	10	じゅっさい	jus-sai
	20	にじゅっさい	ni-jus-sai
	30	さんじゅっさい	san-jus-sai
	70	ななじゅっさい	nana-jus-sai

2. Adjectives

2.1. In Japanese there are two types of adjectives: i-adjectives and na-adjectives. They are so called because of the final syllable (na or i) that is used when they modify nouns.

Examples: きれいな人 kireena hito a pretty woman (na-adjective)
かわいい子ども kawaii kodomo a cute child (i-adjective)

2.2. Adjectives not only modify nouns but also function as predicates. When a sentence contains a predicative adjective, the form of the sentence and the sequence of words in it are the same as in a noun sentence. However, the na of a na-adjective is omitted when it is used as a predicate.

Examples: 鈴木さんは会社員です。
Suzuki-san wa kaishain desu.
Mr. Suzuki is a company employee.

鈴木さんは優しいです。
Suzuki-san wa yasashii desu.
Mr. Suzuki is gentle.

鈴木さんはハンサムなです。
Suzuki-san wa hansamuna desu.
Mr. Suzuki is good-looking.

2.3. The subject is normally omitted when it is self-evident to both the speaker and the listener.

Note: The sentence-final particle ne is used for exclamations.

Examples: きれいですね。　　Kiree desu ne.
　　　　　How beautiful!

　　　　　かわいいですね。　Kawaii desu ne.
　　　　　How cute!

　　　　　大きいですね。　　Ookii desu ne.
　　　　　How big!

　　　　　ハンサムですね。　Hansamu desu ne.
　　　　　How good-looking!

3. ええ、まあ… **Ee, maa**… (Avoiding topics)

→ See Dialogue Ⅰ. Mr. Suzuki does not like talking about his private life. To avoid the topic, he makes his reply short and vague.

✏️ Exercises

1. Substitution drill: Stating age

A：（田中）さんは（40）歳です。　　　　A: (Tanaka)-san wa (40)-sai desu.

例 Ree：田中 Tanaka/40
① 佐藤 Satoo/46　② 鈴木 Suzuki/35　③ 高橋　Takahashi/28

2. Talk about the photos below using the following words.

> ① 妻 tsuma wife, 夫 otto husband, 子ども kodomo child/children
> ② かわいい kawaii cute, ハンサム hansamu good-looking,
> 　きれい kiree beautiful, pretty

A：Bさん、これ、わたしの（① 妻）です。
B：へえ、（② きれい）ですね。

例 Ree：　　　　　　　　　　(1)　　　　　　　　　　(2)

3. Substitution drill: Referring to the pictures, talk about the children.

A：Bさん、これ、わたしの子どもです。
B：へえ、かわいいですね。何歳ですか。
A：（3）歳です。

例 Ree：3　　　　(1) 1　　　　(2) 5

70

 **Fukubukuro**

1. Useful words

Family members

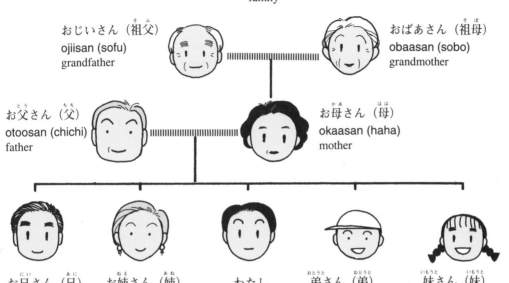

家族
kazoku
family

おじいさん（祖父）
ojiisan (sofu)
grandfather

おばあさん（祖母）
obaasan (sobo)
grandmother

お父さん（父）
otoosan (chichi)
father

お母さん（母）
okaasan (haha)
mother

お兄さん（兄）
oniisan (ani)
older brother

お姉さん（姉）
oneesan (ane)
older sister

わたし
watashi
I

弟さん（弟）
otootosan (otooto)
younger brother

妹さん（妹）
imootosan (imooto)
younger sister

71

ご主人（夫）
go-shujin (otto)
husband

奥さん（妻）
okusan (tsuma)
wife

息子さん（息子）
musukosan (musuko)
son

お嬢さん（娘）
ojoosan (musume)
daughter

your friend
o-tomodachi
my friend
tomodachi

子どもさん（子ども）
kodomosan (kodomo)
child/children

Note: The words in brackets should be used when referring to your own family members.

2. What would you do if... ?

Because of cultural and/or individual differences, favorite or popular topics of conversation vary from one country to another. Check if people in your country like talking about the topics given below. Also, ask for the comments of your classmates and Japanese friends.

· A favorite or popular topic. →(✓)
· An unusual or infrequent topic that should be carefully handled. →(✗)
· Neither of the above. →(?)

·marriage ( )	·sports ( )
·boyfriend(s)/girlfriend(s) ( )	·gossiping ( )
·family ( )	·the arts ( )
·age ( )	·educational background ( )
·weather ( )	·position/status ( )
·salary ( )	·work history ( )
·politics ( )	·sex ( )
·food and drink ( )	·religion ( )
·ethnic group(s) ( )	·social class ( )
·films and plays ( )	·other topics? ( )
·blood type(s) ( )	

5

送る　Okuru

Mailing

写真提供　郵政省

👀 Dialogues

Ⅰ. At the mailing window/Mailing a letter

リ　サ：これ、航空便でお願いします。
局　員：はい。110円になります。

Risa:　　Kore, kookuubin de onegai-
　　　　　shimasu.
Kyokuin: Hai. 110-en ni narimasu.

Lisa:　I would like to send this by airmail.
Clerk:　All right. It's 110 yen.

Ⅱ. At the stamp window/Buying stamps and postcards

リ　サ：150円切手3枚とはがき5枚、
　　　　お願いします。
局　員：ええと、150円切手はありませ
　　　　んので、100円切手と50円切手
　　　　でよろしいですか。
リ　サ：100円と50円。
　　　　str. 2-1, p. 107
局　員：はい。*(He shows her the stamps.)*
リ　サ：はい。いいです。
局　員：700円になります。

Risa:　　150-en kitte 3-mai to hagaki 5-
　　　　　mai, onegai-shimasu.
Kyokuin: Eeto, 150-en kitte wa arimasen
　　　　　node, 100-en kitte to 50-en
　　　　　kitte de yoroshii desu ka.
Risa:　　100-en to 50-en.
　　　　　str. 2-1, p. 107
Kyokuin: Hai. *(He shows her the stamps.)*
Risa:　　Hai. Ii desu.
Kyokuin: 700-en ni narimasu.

Lisa:　Three 150-yen stamps and five
　　　postcards, please.
Clerk:　There are no 150-yen stamps. Can I
　　　make them 100-yen and 50-yen
　　　stamps?
Lisa:　100 yen and 50 yen.
Clerk:　Yes. *(He shows her the stamps.)*
Lisa:　O.K. I'll take them.
Clerk:　700 yen in total.

航空便 kookuubin airmail　〜になります 〜 ni narimasu add up to 〜　切手 kitte stamp　はがき hagaki
postcard　いい ii O.K.

Ⅲ. At the parcel window/Mailing a parcel

リ　サ：これ、フィリピンまで航空便で
　　　　いくらですか。

局　員：ええと、2,150円になります。

リ　サ：2,150円ですね。じゃ、船便だ
　　　　str. 2-1, p. 107
　　　　といくらですか。

局　員：1,500円です。

リ　サ：フィリピンまで船便だとどの
　　　　くらいかかりますか。

局　員：1か月ぐらいですね。

リ　サ：1か月。じゃ、サルだと…
　　　　str. 2-1, p. 107

局　員：1,800円で2週間ぐらいです。

リ　サ：じゃ、サルでお願いします。

局　員：はい。

Risa:	Kore, Firipin made kookuubin de ikura desu ka.
Kyokuin:	Eeto, 2,150-en ni narimasu.
Risa:	2,150-en desu ne. Ja, funabin

str. 2-1, p. 107

da to ikura desu ka.

Kyokuin: 1,500-en desu.

Risa: Firipin made funabin da to donokurai kakarimasu ka.

Kyokuin: 1-kagetsu gurai desu ne.

Risa: 1-kagetsu. Ja, saru da to …

str. 2-1, p. 107

Kyokuin: 1,800-en de 2-shuukan gurai desu.

Risa: Ja, saru de onegai-shimasu.

Kyokuin: Hai.

Lisa: How much will it cost to send this to the Philippines by airmail?

Clerk: Well, it will cost 2,150 yen.

Lisa: 2,150 yen. How much is it if I send it by sea mail?

Clerk: 1,500 yen.

Lisa: How long will it take for this parcel to arrive in the Philippines by sea mail?

Clerk: About a month.

Lisa: A month. If I send it by SAL...

Clerk: It will cost 1,800 yen and take about 2 weeks.

Lisa: I'll send it by SAL, then.

Clerk: O.K.

船便 funabin sea mail　どのくらい donokurai how long　かかります kakarimasu take　1か月 1-kagetsu one month　サル saru SAL　2週間 2-shuukan two weeks

# Grammatical Notes

1. ～でお願いします。 ～ de onegai-shimasu. (Sending mail)

When you are at a post office to mail a letter, try to make yourself understood by using the following expressions.

航空便で	kookuubin de	By airmail,	
船便で	funabin de	By sea mail,	
サルで	saru de	By SAL,	お願いします。
速達で	sokutatsu de	By express,	onegai-shimasu.
書留で	kakitome de	By registered mail,	please.

Example: これ船便でお願いします。

Kore funabin de onegai-shimasu.

By sea mail, please.

2. ～枚 ～-mai (Counter suffix for flat things)

This is used to count flat things such as paper, cloth, plates, dishes and cookies.

いちまい	にまい	さんまい	よんまい	ごまい
ichi-mai	ni-mai	san-mai	yon-mai	go-mai

ろくまい	ななまい	はちまい	きゅうまい	じゅうまい
roku-mai	nana-mai	hachi-mai	kyuu-mai	juu-mai

Its interrogative form is nan-mai.

Examples: はがき5枚ください。

Hagaki 5-mai kudasai.

Five postcards, please.

航空書簡（エアログラム）3枚ください。

Kookuushokan (earoguramu) 3-mai kudasai.

Three aerograms, please.

何枚ですか。

Nan-mai desu ka.

How many pieces/sheets?

速達 sokutatsu express mail　書留 kakitome registered mail　航空書簡 kookuu-shokan aerogram　エアログラム earoguramu aerogram

3. 〜まで〜でいくらですか。 〜 **made** 〜 **de ikura desu ka.** (Asking postage rates)

This expression is useful when you wish to know the postage for sending something to a foreign country by any particular system. The particle **de** is equivalent to 'through' or 'by means of' in English.

Examples:

李　：中国まで航空便でいくらですか。
局　員：1,700円です。
Ri:　　　Chuugoku made kookuubin de ikura desu ka.
Kyokuin: 1,700-en desu.
Li:　　　How much is it if I send this to China by airmail?
Clerk:　1,700 yen.

李：じゃ、航空便でお願いします。
Ri:　Ja, kookuubin de onegai-shimasu.
Li:　I'll send it by airmail, then.

李　：じゃ、船便だといくらですか。
局　員：1,500円です。
李　：じゃ、船便でお願いします。
Ri:　　　Ja, funabin da to ikura desu ka.
Kyokuin: 1,500-en desu.
Ri:　　　Ja, funabin de onegai-shimasu.
Li:　　　How much does it cost if I send it
　　　　by sea mail instead?
Clerk:　1,500 yen.
Li:　　　I'll send it by sea mail, then.

77

Note that **da to**, instead of **de**, is used in the right-hand example. Using **da to**, the whole sentence becomes more conditional. Hence, **funabin da to** means 'If by sea mail.'

4. ～まで～でどのくらいかかりますか。 ～ made ～ de donokurai kakarimasu ka.
(Asking how long something will take by post)

This expression is used when you want to know the time period required for your mail to reach a particular country.

Examples:

> ロバート： アメリカまでサルでどのくらいかかりますか。
> 局　員： 2週間ぐらいです。
>
> Robaato: Amerika made saru de donokurai kakarimasu ka.
> Kyokuin: 2-shuukan gurai desu.
>
> Robert:　How long will it take for this mail to get to the United States if I send it by SAL?
> Clerk:　About two weeks.

> ロバート：じゃ、サルでお願いします。
> Robaato: Ja, saru de onegai-shimasu.
> Robert:　Then I'll send it by SAL.

> ロバート： じゃ、航空便だとどのくらいかかりますか。
> 局　員： 1週間ぐらいです。
> ロバート： じゃ、航空便でお願いします。
>
> Robaato: Ja, kookuubin da to donokurai kakarimasu ka.
> Kyokuin: 1-shuukan gurai desu.
> Robaato: Ja, kookuubin de onegai-shimasu.
>
> Robert:　If I send it by airmail instead, how long will it take?
> Clerk:　About a week.
> Robert:　If that's the case, I'll send it by airmail.

In the second example here, like in 3 on the previous page, da to is used in place of de.

Exercises

1. Substitution drill: Sending letters

A：これ、（航空便）でお願いします。　　　　A: Kore, (kookuubin) de onegai-shimasu.

例 Ree : airmail　(1) express mail　(2) sea mail　　　(3) registered mail

2. Substitution drill: Buying stamps and aerograms

あなた：（80円切手）、（2）枚 お願いします。　Anata:　(80-en kitte), (2)-mai onegai-
局　員：はい。（160）円です。　　　　　　　　　　　　shimasu.
　　　　　　　　　　　　　　　　　　　　　　　　　　Kyokuin: Hai. (160)-en desu.

例 Ree : two 80-yen stamps
(1) eight 50-yen stamps　　(2) five 270-yen stamps　　(3) three aerograms at 90 yen each

3. Using the postage table, make up a dialogue concerning the best method of sending things under the following conditions.

Example: You want to send a 2-kilogram parcel to China so that you can receive it yourself two
weeks later on your return to China.

あなた：これ、中国まで航空便でいくら　　　Anata:　Kore, Chuugoku made kookuubin
　　　　ですか。　　　　　　　　　　　　　　　　　de ikura desu ka.
局　員：2,750円です。　　　　　　　　　　　Kyokuin: 2,750-en desu.
あなた：じゃ、船便だといくらですか。　　　Anata:　Ja, funabin da to ikura desu ka.
局　員：1,750円です。　　　　　　　　　　　Kyokuin: 1,750-en desu.
あなた：これ、中国まで船便でどのくら　　　Anata:　Kore, Chuugoku made funabin de
　　　　いかかりますか。　　　　　　　　　　　　donokurai kakarimasu ka.
局　員：1か月ぐらいです。　　　　　　　　　Kyokuin: 1-kagetsu gurai desu.
あなた：そうですか。航空便だとどのく　　　Anata:　Soo desu ka. Kookuubin da to
　　　　らいかかりますか。　　　　　　　　　　　donokurai kakarimasu ka.
局　員：1週間ぐらいです。　　　　　　　　　Kyokuin: 1-shuukan gurai desu.
あなた：じゃ、航空便でお願いします。　　　Anata:　Ja, kookuubin de onegai-shimasu.

(1) You want to send a Christmas gift weighing 400 grams to a relative in Brazil. Christmas is one month away. Start your dialogue with the following sentence.

あなた：これ、ブラジルまで航空便でいくらですか。
Anata: Kore, Burajiru made kookuubin de ikura desu ka.

(2) You want to send something to your home country. Make up your own dialogue concerning the weight of the parcel, when it has to arrive in your country and the method of delivery you want to use.

航空便 kookuubin airmail (takes a week)   (issued on July 6, 1998)

	East Asia	Southeast Asia/ Southwest Asia	North and Central America/Oceania/ West Asia/Europe	South America/ Africa
Less than 500 g	1,700 yen	2,100 yen	2,500 yen	3,200 yen
500 g and over but less than 5 kg	Increase by 350 yen for every additional 500 g	Increase by 600 yen for every additional 500 g	Increase by 850 yen for every additional 500 g	Increase by 1,400 yen for every additional 500 g
5 kg and over but less than 10 kg	Increase by 300 yen for every additional 500 g	Increase by 500 yen for every additional 500 g	Increase by 750 yen for every additional 500 g	Increase by 1,200 yen for every additional 500 g
10 kg and over	Increase by 400 yen for every additional 1 kg	Increase by 700 yen for every additional 1 kg	Increase by 950 yen for every additional 1 kg	Increase by 1,600 yen for every additional 1 kg

船便 funabin sea mail (takes a month)

	East Asia	Southeast Asia/ Southwest Asia	North and Central America/Oceania/ West Asia/Europe	South America/ Africa
Less than 1 kg	1,500 yen	1,700 yen	1,800 yen	2,200 yen
1 kg and over but less than 10 kg	Increase by 250 yen for every additional 1 kg	Increase by 400 yen for every additional 1 kg	Increase by 550 yen for every additional 1 kg	Increase by 450 yen for every additional 1 kg
10 kg and over	Increase by 200 yen for every additional 1 kg	Increase by 300 yen for every additional 1 kg	Increase by 350 yen for every additional 1 kg	Increase by 350 yen for every additional 1 kg

![福] Fukubukuro

Post office information

1. Post office windows

There are two types of windows at the post office.

A 切手 kitte stamps 　小包 kozutsumi parcels 　郵便 yuubin mail	B 貯金 chokin savings 　為替 kawase postal giro 　保険 hoken insurance 　振替 furikae postal transfer

Which window do you use when you want to:

(1) send a parcel to Brazil?

(2) send registered mail?

(3) send money by postal giro?

2. Mailboxes

Mailboxes in Japan usually have two slots. In Tokyo, mail is divided into two groups:

　　a. ordinary domestic letters and postcards

　　b. express mail, international mail, and others

Check with the mailboxes in the area where you live. When you are sending the following types of mail, which slot is the right one?

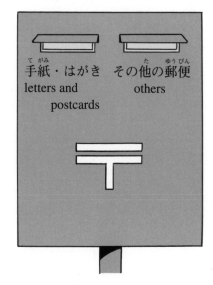

(1) domestic express mail

(2) aerograms

(3) domestic postcards

(4) domestic book mail

(5) letters to your country

3. SAL

SAL is a system for sending parcels abroad that is faster than sea mail but cheaper than airmail.

When you would like to ask a clerk if your parcel can be sent by SAL or not, say the following:

(name of country)までサルで送れますか。

(name of country) made saru de okuremasu ka.

Can I send this to (name of country) by SAL?

4. Business hours

Opening days and hours differ between ordinary and major post offices. Opening hours are also different between the windows for mail and those for financial transactions. Check with the opening hours of the post office near your home.

Language Focus **Time Expressions**

1. ～時 ~-ji (~ o'clock)

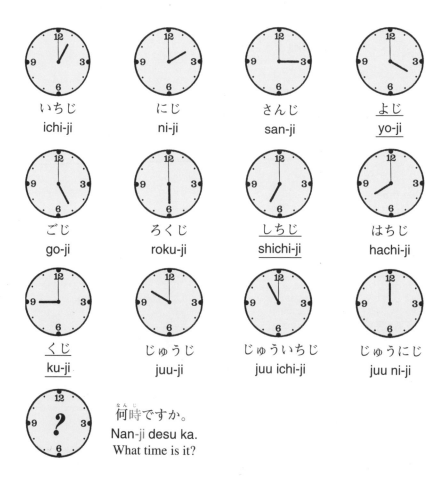

いちじ	にじ	さんじ	<u>よじ</u>
ichi-ji	ni-ji	san-ji	yo-ji
ごじ	ろくじ	<u>しちじ</u>	はちじ
go-ji	roku-ji	shichi-ji	hachi-ji
<u>くじ</u>	じゅうじ	じゅういちじ	じゅうにじ
ku-ji	juu-ji	juu ichi-ji	juu ni-ji

何時ですか。
Nan-ji desu ka.
What time is it?

Note: Be careful in pronouncing the underlined numbers.

2. ～分 ~-fun (~ minute)

The Chinese character '分' is pronounced either fun or pun depending on the preceding sound.

	いっ	さん	よん	ろっ	はっ	じゅっ	
	1	3	4	6	8	10	分
1 時	ip	san	yon	rop	hap	jup	-pun
1-ji	に		ご	なな	きゅう		分
	2		5	7	9		-fun
	ni		go	nana	kyuu		

Examples: 4:20   4時20分 yo-ji ni-jup-pun
5:15   5時15分 go-ji juu go-fun

3. ～時半 **～-ji han** (half past ～)

Example: 1:30 1時半 ichi-ji han

4. 午前／午後 **gozen/gogo** (a.m./p.m.)

Examples: 1 a.m. 午前1時 gozen ichi-ji
2 p.m. 午後2時 gogo ni-ji

5. Asking the time

A：あの、ちょっとすみません。今、何時ですか。　A: Ano, chotto sumimasen. Ima, nan-ji desu ka.
B：ええと…、3時です。　B: Eeto…, 3-ji desu.
A：3時ですね。どうも。　A: 3-ji desu ne. Doomo.
B：いいえ。　B: Iie.

A: Excuse me. What time is it now?
B: Well... It's 3 o'clock.
A: 3 o'clock. Thank you.
B: You're welcome.

Language Focus **Periods of Time**

1. ～分 ［間］ **～-fun[kan]** (for ～ minutes)

Examples:

10分 ［間］ jup-pun[kan] (10 minutes)

5分 ［間］ go-fun[kan] (5 minutes)

2. ～時間 **～-jikan** (for ～ hours)

Examples:

2 時間 ni-jikan (2 hours)

3 時間 san-jikan (3 hours)

3. ～か月 **～-kagetsu** (for ～ months)

Example:

3 か月 san-kagetsu (3 months)

1							2							3						
日	月	火	水	木	金	土	日	月	火	水	木	金	土	日	月	火	水	木	金	土
1	2	3	4	5	6	7					1	2	3					1	2	3
8	9	10	11	12	13	14	5	6	7	8	9	10	11	5	6	7	8	9	10	11
15	16	17	18	19	20	21	12	13	14	15	16	17	18	12	13	14	15	16	17	18
22	23	24	25	26	27	28	19	20	21	22	23	24	25	19	20	21	22	23	24	25
29	30	31					26	27	28					26	27	28	29	30	31	

4. 〜週間 〜-shuukan, 〜日 〜-nichi (for 〜 weeks, 〜 days)

Examples:

5

日	月	火	水	木	金	土
	1	2	3	4	5	6
7	8	9	10	11	12	13
14	15	16	17	18	19	20
21	22	23	24	25	26	27
28	29	30	31			

2週間 ni-shuukan (2 weeks)

1日 ichi-nichi (1 day)

2日[間] futsuka[-kan] (2 days)

5. Asking how long

A：東京から大阪までどのくらいかかりますか。
B：3時間です。

A: Tookyoo kara Oosaka made donokurai kakarimasu ka.
B: 3-jikan desu.

A: How long does it take from Tokyo to Osaka?
B: It takes 3 hours.

86

6

でんわ
電話する　Denwa-suru

Phoning

 **Dialogues**

Ⅰ. Calling a friend at work

受 付：はい、東京コンピュータです。

マリオ：あの、李さん、お願いします。
受 付：あの、失礼ですが…
マリオ：あっ、マリオと申します。

マリオ：あの、マリオと申しますが、
　　　　李さん、お願いします。

受 付：はい、少々お待ちください。

李：もしもし、李です。

受 付：あの、すみません、李はきょう、休みです。
マリオ：ああ、そうですか。じゃ、結構です。
　　　　どうも。失礼します。
受 付：失礼します。

Uketsuke: Hai, Tookyoo-konpyuuta desu.

Mario:　　Ano, Ri-san, onegai-shimasu.
Uketsuke: Ano, shitsuree desu ga…
Mario:　　A, Mario to mooshimasu.

Mario: Ano, Mario to mooshimasu ga,
　　　　Ri-san, onegai-shimasu.

Uketsuke: Hai, shooshoo o-machi kudasai.

Ri: Moshimoshi, Ri desu.

Uketsuke: Ano, sumimasen, Ri wa kyoo,
　　　　yasumi desu.
Mario:　　Aa, soo desu ka. Ja, kekkoo desu.
　　　　Doomo. Shitsuree-shimasu.
Uketsuke: Shitsuree-shimasu.

88

コンピュータ konpyuuta computer　お願いします onegai-shimasu please　失礼ですが… Shitsuree desu ga… Excuse me (may I have your name?)　～と申しますが　～ to mooshimasu ga　My name is... 少々 shooshoo a moment　お待ちください。O-machi kudasai. Hold on, please.

Receptionist: Tokyo Computers. Can I help you?

Mario: Can I speak to Ms. Li, please?
Receptionist: May I have your name?
Mario: Oh, sorry. My name is Mario.

Mario: My name is Mario.
       Can I speak to Ms. Li, please?

Receptionist: Hold on, please.

Li: Hello. Li speaking.

Receptionist: I'm afraid Ms. Li is off today.
Mario: I see. All right, then. Thank you.
Receptionist: Goodbye.

もしもし。 Moshimoshi. Hello. きょう kyoo today 休み yasumi day off/absence 結構です。 Kekkoo desu. All right. 失礼します。 Shitsuree-shimasu. Goodbye.

Ⅱ. Calling a friend at home

かおりの母：　はい。
マ　リ　オ：　高橋さんのお宅ですか。
かおりの母：　はい、そうです。
マ　リ　オ：　マリオと申しますが、かおりさん、いらっしゃいますか。

かおりの母：　マリオさんですか。
マ　リ　オ：　はい。
かおりの母：　少々お待ちください。
マ　リ　オ：　はい、お願いします。

かおりの母：　かおりは、今、いませんが…
マ　リ　オ：　ああ、そうですか。
　　　　　　　じゃ、結構です。どうも。
str. 5-2, p. 107

か　お　り：　もしもし、かおりです。

Kaori no haha: Hai.
Mario:　　　　Takahashi-san no otaku desu ka.
Kaori no haha: Hai, soo desu.
Mario:　　　　Mario to mooshimasu ga, Kaori-san, irasshaimasu ka.

Kaori no haha: Mario-san desu ka.
Mario:　　　　Hai.
Kaori no haha: Shooshoo o-machi
　　　　　　　kudasai.
Mario:　　　　Hai, onegai-shimasu.

Kaori no haha: Kaori wa, ima, imasen ga ⋯
Mario:　　　　Aa, soo desu ka. Ja, kekkoo
　　　　　　　desu. Doomo.
str. 5-2, p. 107

Kaori: Moshimoshi, Kaori desu.

お宅 otaku somebody else's home　いらっしゃいます irasshaimasu <respectful form of imasu>　今 ima now
います imasu be present

Kaori's mother: Hello.
Mario: Is this Ms. Takahashi's home?
Kaori's mother: Yes.
Mario: My name is Mario. Can I speak to Kaori, please?

Kaori's mother: Mario, did you say?
Mario: That's right.
Kaori's mother: Hold on, please.
Mario: Yes.

Kaori's mother: Kaori is out now.
Mario: Is she? All right. Thank you.

Kaori: Hello. Kaori speaking.

☺ Grammatical Notes

1. ～さん、お願いします。 ～-san, onegai-shimasu. (Mr./Ms. ～, please)

This is an expression for asking to be put through to someone.

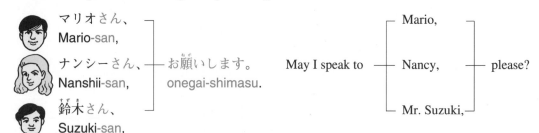

マリオさん、 Mario-san,		Mario,	
ナンシーさん、 Nanshii-san,	お願いします。 onegai-shimasu.	May I speak to	Nancy,	please?
鈴木さん、 Suzuki-san,		Mr. Suzuki,	

2. ～と申しますが ～ to mooshimasu ga (My name is ～.)

This is a way for you to give your name on the phone.

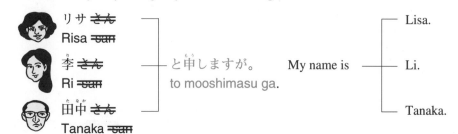

リサ さん Risa ~san~		Lisa.
李 さん Ri ~san~	と申しますが。 to mooshimasu ga.	My name is	Li.
田中 さん Tanaka ~san~		Tanaka.

92

3. ～さん、いらっしゃいますか。 ～-san, irasshaimasu ka. (Is Mr./Ms. ～ in?)

This is a typical expression for asking if someone is there.

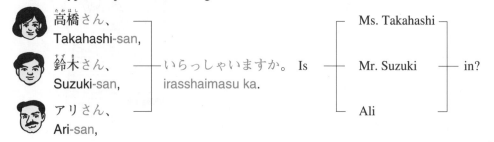

高橋さん、 Takahashi-san,		Ms. Takahashi	
鈴木さん、 Suzuki-san,	いらっしゃいますか。 irasshaimasu ka.	Is	Mr. Suzuki	in?
アリさん、 Ari-san,		Ali	

4. Omission of -san

When you are referring to someone in your family or someone within your company, -san should not be used.

Example: あの、すみません。李~~さん~~は、きょう休みです。

Ano, sumimasen. Ri ~~san~~ wa, kyoo yasumi desu.

Ms. Li is off today.

5. 失礼ですが… **Shitsuree desu ga… (Asking someone's name)**

The above is a shortened form of 'Shitsuree desu ga, dochira-sama deshoo ka (May I have your name, please?),' but some Japanese people prefer to use the above abbreviated form.

6. 少々、お待ちください。 **Shooshoo, o-machi kudasai. (Please wait a moment.)**

In conversation, people usually say 'Chotto matte kudasai (Wait a moment),' but in order to be polite, 'shooshoo (for a moment)' is used instead of chotto, and 'o-machi kudasai (Would you please wait?),' an honorific form of matte kudasai, is preferred.

7. もしもし。 **Moshimoshi. (Hello.)**

This means 'hello' and is used as a greeting on the phone.

8. じゃ、結構です。 **Ja, kekkoo desu. (Oh, O.K.)**

Kekkoo desu means 'good' or 'enough' or 'O.K.' When a Japanese uses this expression on being informed that the person he/she would like to speak to is not in, it implies that he/she has no particular message to leave.

✎ Exercises

1. **Imagine you are calling a friend at his company. Insert one of the names below in [ ] and your name in < >. Practice situations (1) and (2). If a friend is with you right now, role-play (A and B) with him or her for practice.**

例 Ree：李 Ri ① ナンシー Nanshii ② リサ Risa ③ 鈴木 Suzuki

A：はい、東京コンピュータです。
B：あの、[李]さん、お願いします。
A：あの、失礼ですが…
B：あっ、<マリオ>と申します。
A：はい、少々お待ちください。

      (1)   (2)

C：もしもし、[李]です。

A：あの、すみません。[李]は、きょう、休みです。
B：ああ、そうですか。じゃ、結構です。
　　どうも。失礼します。
A：失礼します。

A: Hai, Tookyoo-konpyuuta desu.
B: Ano, [Ri]-san, onegai-shimasu.
A: Ano, shitsuree desu ga…
B: A, <Mario> to mooshimasu.
A: Hai, shooshoo o-machi kudasai.

      (1)   (2)

C: Moshimoshi, [Ri] desu.

A: Ano, sumimasen.
　 [Ri] wa, kyoo, yasumi desu.
B: Aa, soo desu ka. Ja, kekkoo desu.
　 Doomo. Shitsuree-shimasu.
A: Shitsuree-shimasu.

94

2. Now call a Japanese friend. Insert his/her family name in [ ] and his/her first name in ( ). And your name should be inserted in < >. Practice situations (1) and (2). If you happen to be with a friend now, role-play with him or her for practice.

	family name	first name	family name	first name
例 Ree :	高橋	かおり	Takahashi	Kaori
①	佐藤	和子	Satoo	Kazuko
②	田中	一郎	Tanaka	Ichiroo
③	鈴木	洋平	Suzuki	Yoohee

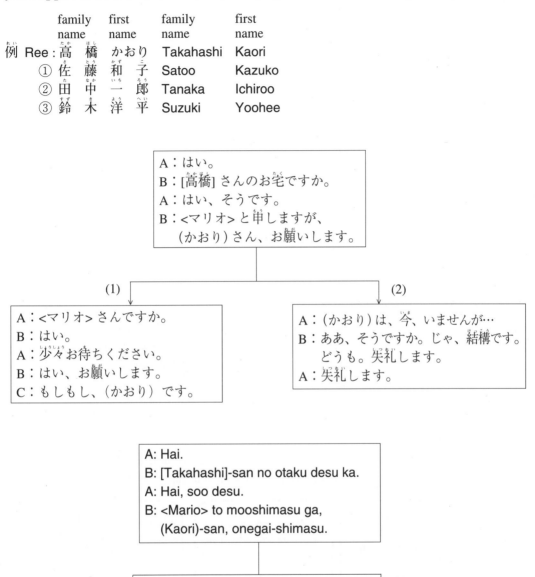

A：はい。
B：[高橋] さんのお宅ですか。
A：はい、そうです。
B：＜マリオ＞と申しますが、
　（かおり）さん、お願いします。

(1)
A：＜マリオ＞さんですか。
B：はい。
A：少々お待ちください。
B：はい、お願いします。
C：もしもし、（かおり）です。

(2)
A：（かおり）は、今、いませんが…
B：ああ、そうですか。じゃ、結構です。
　どうも。失礼します。
A：失礼します。

A: Hai.
B: [Takahashi]-san no otaku desu ka.
A: Hai, soo desu.
B: <Mario> to mooshimasu ga,
　(Kaori)-san, onegai-shimasu.

(1)
A: <Mario>-san desu ka.
B: Hai.
A: Shooshoo o-machi kudasai.
B: Hai, onegai-shimasu.
C: Moshimoshi, (Kaori) desu.

(2)
A: (Kaori) wa, ima, imasen ga…
B: Aa, soo desu ka. Ja, kekkoo desu.
　Doomo. Shitsuree-shimasu.
A: Shitsuree-shimasu.

95

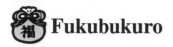 **Fukubukuro**

1. Katakana

Match the Japanese and English words.

例 Ree : テレホンカード　terehon-kaado　・　・① button
　　(1) ランプ　　　　　ranpu　　　　・　・② dial
　　(2) ボタン　　　　　botan　　　　・　・③ telephone card
　　(3) ダイヤル　　　　daiyaru　　　・　・④ lamp

2. Chinese characters

Basic meaning

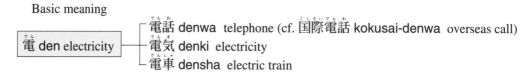

電 den electricity ┌ 電話 denwa　telephone (cf. 国際電話 kokusai-denwa　overseas call)
　　　　　　　　├ 電気 denki　electricity
　　　　　　　　└ 電車 densha　electric train

3. Puzzle

Match the telephone number with the service.

例 Ree : 110 ・　・① 時報　　　　　jihoo　　　　　　the time
　(1) 119 ・　・② 電話番号　　　denwa-bangoo　directory enquiries
　(2) 104 ・　・③ 警察　　　　　keesatsu　　　　police department
　(3) 117 ・　・④ 天気予報　　　tenki-yohoo　　weather report
　(4) 177 ・　・⑤ 消防署、　　　shooboosho,　　fire department,
　　　　　　　　　　救急車　　　　kyuukyuusha　ambulance service

4. What would you do if...?

Have you found any difference in customs and practices concerning telephone calls between your country and Japan? Talk about the following topics with your Japanese and non-Japanese friends.

What time of night do you think is the latest that you can make a phone call without being rude?

When you are going to be late for work, do you normally call the company to notify your colleagues or boss?

When you are talking on the phone and cannot see the person with whom you are speaking, is it proper to say 'yes,' 'uhhuh' or 'well' very frequently in order to show that you are listening?

When you meet someone for the first time, is it unusual to ask for their phone number?

Are you supposed to start speaking on the phone by giving your name first?

7

移動する　Idoo-suru

Traveling

 **Dialogues**

Ⅰ. At a station/Asking the destination of a train

(Ms. Li is at Ochanomizu Station and wants to go to Shinjuku.)

李　：すみません、これ、新宿行き
　　　ますか。

駅　員：え？
　　　str. 1-1, p. 106

李　：新宿。
　　　str. 4-1, p. 107

駅　員：ああ、新宿、行きますよ。

李　：あ、どうも。

Ri: Sumimasen, kore, Shinjuku
ikimasu ka.

Ekiin: E?
str. 1-1, p. 106

Ri: Shinjuku.
str. 4-1, p. 107

Ekiin: Aa, Shinjuku, ikimasu yo.

Ri: A, doomo.

Li: Excuse me. Does this
train go to Shinjuku?

Station employee: What?

Li: Shinjuku.

Station employee: Oh, Shinjuku. Yes, it
does.

Li: Thank you.

新宿 Shinjuku Shinjuku　行きます ikimasu go　どうも。Doomo. Thank you.

II. At a station/Asking if a train stops at a particular station

(Ms. Li is at Ochanomizu Station and wants to go to Okubo.)

李 ：すみません、これ大久保に止まりますか。

駅員：大久保、ええと、これは快速ですから止まりませんよ。

李 ：止まりません？
str. 1-6, p. 106

駅員：そう、各駅停車に乗って。

李 ：かくえき…？
str. 1-5, p. 106

駅員：そう、あの黄色い電車。

李 ：あ、はい、どうも。

Ri: Sumimasen, kore Ookubo ni tomarimasu ka.

Ekiin: Ookubo, eeto, kore wa kaisoku desu kara tomarimasen yo.

Ri: Tomarimasen?
str. 1-6, p. 106

Ekiin: Soo, kakueki-teesha ni notte.

Ri: Kakueki…?
str. 1-5, p. 106

Ekiin: Soo, ano kiiroi densha.

Ri: A, hai, doomo.

Li: Excuse me. Does this train stop at Okubo?

Station employee: Okubo... Well, this is a rapid-service train so it doesn't stop there.

Li: Doesn't stop there?

Station employee: No, it doesn't. You should take a local train.

Li: Local...

Station employee: Yes, that yellow one.

Li: Oh, I see. Thank you.

99

大久保 Ookubo Okubo 止まります tomarimasu stop 快速 kaisoku rapid-service train 各駅停車 kakueki-teesha local train 黄色い kiiroi yellow 電車 densha train

Ⅲ. In a train/Checking the station

(Ms. Li is on a Chuo Line train going to Okubo.)

李 ：	すみません、ここ、どこですか。
乗 客：	ええと、ここは代々木。
李 ：	大久保はまだですか。
乗 客：	ええ、あと５分くらい。
李 ：	いくつめですか。
乗 客：	ええと、１つ、２つ…大久保は２つめ。
李 ：	すみません、大久保で教えてください。
乗 客：	ええ、いいですよ。
李 ：	どうも。

Ri:	Sumimasen, koko, doko desu ka.
Jookyaku:	Eeto, koko wa Yoyogi.
Ri:	Ookubo wa mada desu ka.
Jookyaku:	Ee, ato 5-fun kurai.
Ri:	Ikutsu-me desu ka.
Jookyaku:	Eeto, hitotsu, futatsu… Ookubo wa futatsu-me.
Ri:	Sumimasen, Ookubo de oshiete kudasai.
Jookyaku:	Ee, ii desu yo.
Ri:	Doomo.

Li:	Excuse me. Where are we now?
Passenger:	We are now at Yoyogi.
Li:	So we haven't arrived at Okubo yet?
Passenger:	Perhaps in five minutes.
Li:	How many more stations?
Passenger:	Well, one, two... Okubo is the second station after this.
Li:	Would you be kind enough to tell me when the train arrives at Okubo?
Passenger:	Sure.
Li:	Thank you.

100

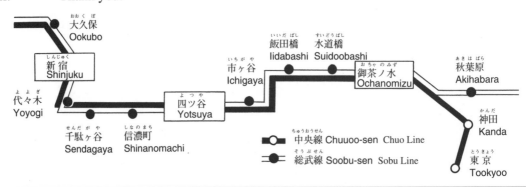

ここ koko here　どこ doko where　代々木 Yoyogi Yoyogi　まだ mada not yet　あと ato another　２つめ futatsu-me the second　教えてください。 Oshiete kudasai. Please tell me.

Grammatical Notes

1. Verbs

	Present affirmative	Present negative	In a sentence
	行きます ikimasu	行きません ikimasen	(place) に／へ行きます (place) ni/e ikimasu
	乗ります norimasu	乗りません norimasen	(train, car, etc.)に乗ります (train, car, etc.) ni norimasu
	止まります tomarimasu	止まりません tomarimasen	(place)に止まります (place) ni tomarimasu

Note: Verbs in Japanese are used with particles (e.g., ni, e, etc.), but these may be omitted in daily conversation.

2. ～め ～-me (Suffix for ordinal numbers)

This is used to count or ask the number of stations to one's destination. The number includes the destination itself.

Question form: 大久保はいくつめですか。

Ookubo wa ikutsu-me desu ka.

How many more stations from here to Okubo?

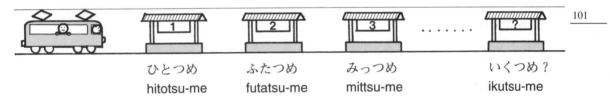

ひとつめ	ふたつめ	みっつめ	いくつめ？
hitotsu-me	futatsu-me	mittsu-me	ikutsu-me

In such expressions, -me (which means -th) is added to the end of hitotsu (one), futatsu (two), mittsu (three), etc.

3. ～から ～ kara (Giving reasons)

Kara is used to indicate reasons. It can also be used to combine two sentences. In the following example, 'This is a rapid service train' and 'It doesn't stop there' have been combined into one sentence using kara.

Example: これは快速ですから、止まりませんよ。

Kore wa kaisoku desu kara, tomarimasen yo.

This is a rapid-service train, so it doesn't stop there.

 **Exercises**

1. Look at the pictures below and fill in each blank with the correct word.

Words: 行きます ikimasu　乗ります norimasu　止まります tomarimasu

(1) (　　　　　　) 　(2) (　　　　　　) 　(3) (　　　　　　)

2. Make questions and give affirmative and negative answers using the following verbs.

例：行きます → Question（行きますか）。→ はい、（行きます）。／いいえ、（行きません）。

Ree : ikimasu → Question (Ikimasu ka). → Hai, (ikimasu). ／Iie, (ikimasen).

(1) 止まります → (　　　　　　)。
　→ はい、(　　　　　　)。／いいえ、(　　　　　　)。
　tomarimasu → (　　　　　)．
　→ Hai,(　　　　　)．/Iie,(　　　　　)．

(2) 乗ります→ (　　　　　)。
　→ はい、(　　　　　)。／いいえ、(　　　　　)。
　norimasu → (　　　　)．
　→ Hai,(　　　　)． /Iie,(　　　　)．

3. Substitution drill:

(1) Asking if a train goes to a specific station

A：すみません。　　　　　　　　　　A: Sumimasen.
　これ、(新宿)、行きますか。　　　　Kore, (Shinjuku), ikimasu ka.
B：はい、行きます。／　　　　　　　B: Hai, ikimasu./
　いいえ、行きません。　　　　　　　Iie, ikimasen.
A：あ、どうも。　　　　　　　　　　A: A, doomo.

例 Ree：新宿 Shinjuku　① 渋谷 Shibuya　② 東京 Tookyoo　③ 川崎 Kawasaki

(2) Asking if a train stops at a specific station

A：すみません。　　　　　　　　　　A: Sumimasen.
　これ、(大久保) に、止まりますか。　Kore, (Ookubo) ni, tomarimasu ka.
B：はい、止まります。／　　　　　　B: Hai, tomarimasu./
　いいえ、止まりません。　　　　　　Iie, tomarimasen.
A：あ、どうも。　　　　　　　　　　A: A, doomo.

例 Ree：大久保 Ookubo　① 中野 Nakano　② 新宿 Shinjuku　③ 横浜 Yokohama

4. Look at the train line map. Imagine you are on your way to Okubo but do not know how many stations there are from where you are now. Using -me, practice asking how many stops there are to your destination.

例 Ree : You are at Yoyogi.

A：大久保はいくつめですか。　　　A: Ookubo wa ikutsu-me desu ka.
B：（2つ）めです。　　　　　　　B: (Futatsu)-me desu.

Make questions and answers relevant to the following situations.

(1) You are now at Suidobashi and on your way to Okubo.
(2) You are now at Yotsuya and on your way to Okubo.
(3) You are now at Ichigaya and on your way to Okubo.

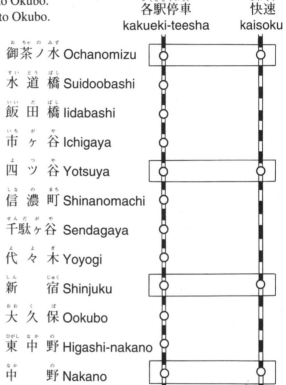

各駅停車　　　快速
kakueki-teesha　　kaisoku

御茶ノ水 Ochanomizu
水道橋 Suidoobashi
飯田橋 Iidabashi
市ヶ谷 Ichigaya
四ツ谷 Yotsuya
信濃町 Shinanomachi
千駄ヶ谷 Sendagaya
代々木 Yoyogi
新宿 Shinjuku
大久保 Ookubo
東中野 Higashi-nakano
中野 Nakano

103

5. Look at the train line map for Exercise 4. Say whether a train stops at a specific station or not and use kara to give the reason.

A：これ大久保に止まりますか。　　A: Kore Ookubo ni tomarimasu ka.
B：いいえ、快速ですから、止まりませんよ。　B: Iie, kaisoku desu kara, tomarimasen yo.

(1) 各駅停車 kakueki-teesha (local train)
　　A：これ大久保に止まりますか。　　A: Kore Ookubo ni tomarimasu ka.
　　B：（　　　　　　　　　）B: (　　　　　　　　　　　　　　　　)

(2) 快速 kaisoku (rapid-service train)
　　A：これ代々木に止まりますか。　　A: Kore Yoyogi ni tomarimasu ka.
　　B：（　　　　　　　　　）B: (　　　　　　　　　　　　　　　　)

(3) 快速 kaisoku (rapid-service train)
　　A：これ水道橋に止まりますか。　　A: Kore Suidoobashi ni tomarimasu ka.
　　B：（　　　　　　　　　）B: (　　　　　　　　　　　　　　　　)

 **Fukubukuro**

1. Puzzle (What is the name of this station?)

例 Ree : (④)   (1) (   )   (2) (   )   (3) (   )

新宿 しんじゅく	渋谷 しぶや	東京 とうきょう	川崎 かわさき

① Shibuya ② Kawasaki ③ Tokyo ④ Shinjuku

2. Types of trains

There are local and non-local trains. Local trains stop at every station, while non-local ones do not. So you have to be careful when you get on a train. Non-local trains may have different names depending on the line.

中央線 Chuuoo-sen Chuo Line:

特別快速 tokubetsu-kaisoku
　　　　special rapid-service

快速 kaisoku rapid-service

各駅停車 kakueki-teesha local

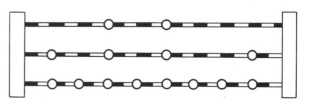

京王線 Keeoo-sen Keio Line:

特急 tokkyuu limited express

急行 kyuukoo express

快速 kaisoku rapid-service

各駅停車 kakueki-teesha local

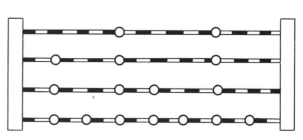

小田急線 Odakyuu-sen Odakyu Line:

特急 tokkyuu limited express

急行 kyuukoo express

準急 junkyuu semi-express

各駅停車 kakueki-teesha local

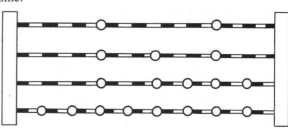

104

3. Useful signs

Match each sign with its reading and then identify its meaning.

例 Ree : (⑥) (b)　　　(1) ( ) ( )

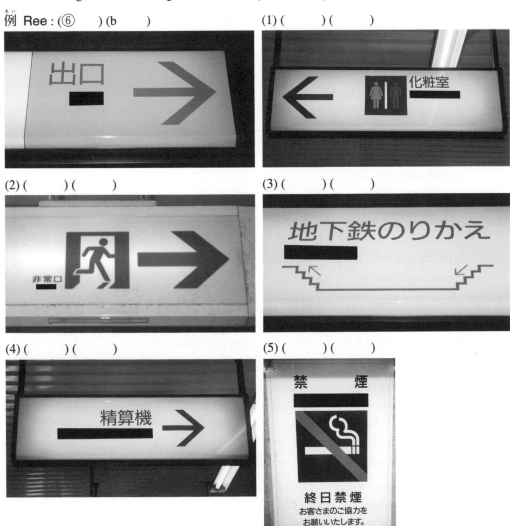

(2) ( ) ( )　　　(3) ( ) ( )

(4) ( ) ( )　　　(5) ( ) ( )

---

① hijooguchi　② keshooshitsu　③ seesanki　④ kin'en
⑤ chikatetsu norikae　⑥ deguchi

---

a. Transfer to Subway　b. Exit　c. Fare Adjustment Machines
d. No Smoking　e. Rest Rooms　f. Emergency Exit

Language Focus **Summary of Strategies**

When you cannot express yourself in Japanese, or when you do not understand what a Japanese is saying to you, you should try using one of the following strategies. You will find them useful.

1. When you do not understand what a person is saying

1-1 When you cannot hear what he or she is saying to you:

え？ E? Pardon me?

1-2 When you cannot understand what he or she is saying to you:

すみません、わかりません。

Sumimasen, wakarimasen.

Sorry, but I don't understand.

1-3 When you would like to ask him or her to repeat what they said:

すみません、もう一度お願いします。

Sumimasen, moo ichido onegai-shimasu.

Would you repeat that, please?

1-4 When you would like to ask him or her to speak slowly:

すみません、もう少しゆっくりお願いします。

Sumimasen, moo sukoshi yukkuri onegai-shimasu.

Would you speak a little more slowly, please?

1-5 When you do not understand the meaning of any word or phrase:

すみません、〜って何ですか。

Sumimasen, 〜tte nan desu ka.

Excuse me, what is the meaning of 〜 ?

Or you should repeat the word or phrase with a rising intonation.

1-6 When you are hearing the answer to a question which should start with 'hai (yes)' or 'iie (no),' pay attention to whether the answer is positive or negative and also to the verb that is used. It is advisable to confirm the answer by asking the question in a different way.

You:	新宿、行きますか。	Shinjuku, ikimasu ka.	Is (this train) going to Shinjuku?
Japanese:	… ? … ? … ? …	…?…?…?…	...?...?...?...
You:	新宿、行きません？	Shinjuku, ikimasen?	It's not going to Shinjuku?

1-7 When you would like to know the meaning of a particular word or phrase.

〜ってどういう意味ですか。

〜tte dooiu imi desu ka.

What do you mean by 〜 ?

〜って英語／〜語で何ですか。

〜tte eego/〜-go de nan desu ka.

What is the English/(other language) for 〜 ?

2. To confirm what a person is saying to you

2-1 When you are hearing something that is highly important to you, such as a physician's explanation about the dosage of a medicine, you should make sure whether your understanding is correct or not by repeating what he or she said and adding 'desu ne? (right?)' at the end.

2-2 In order to indicate that you are listening, give some responses occasionally, saying 'hai (yes)' or 'ee (yeah),' or by nodding.

3. When you have difficulty in making yourself understood in Japanese

3-1 When you are thinking what to say and how to say it while speaking, such words as 'eeto (er-r)' or 'ano (well)' can be used as sentence fillers.

3-2 When you would like to know how to say any particular word or phrase in Japanese:

　〜は日本語で何て言いますか。

　〜 wa Nihon-go de nan te iimasu ka.

　How do you say 〜 in Japanese?

3-3 You could try using another Japanese word with a similar meaning. /You could try explaining in Japanese anyway.

3-4 Use body language./Draw a picture./Write Chinese characters.

3-5 Use another language.

4. When a Japanese does not understand your Japanese

4-1 You should repeat what you said slowly./You should slowly pronounce only the word that you think is important.

4-2 Try and say it another way.

　Example: 熱 netsu (fever) - 熱い atsui (hot)

5. How to start and finish conversations

5-1 When you wish to gain someone's attention:

　すみません。Sumimasen. Excuse me.

5-2 When you wish to finish a conversation:

　どうも。Doomo. Thank you.

Example dialogues
Dialogue Ⅰ:

李 ：<u>すみません</u>。これ、新宿に行きます
str. 5-1 Attracting attention
か。

駅員：<u>え？</u>
str. 1-1 Indicating incomprehension

李 ：<u>新宿</u>。
str. 4-1 Repeating

駅員：ああ、新宿。行きますよ。

李 ：<u>あ、どうも</u>。
str. 5-2 Winding up a conversation

Ri: <u>Sumimasen</u>. Kore, Shinjuku ni ikimasu
str. 5-1 Attracting attention
ka.

Ekiin: <u>E?</u>
str. 1-1 Indicating incomprehension

Ri: <u>Shinjuku.</u>
str. 4-1 Repeating

Ekiin: Aa, Shinjuku. Ikimasu yo.

Ri: <u>A, doomo.</u>
str. 5-2 Winding up a conversation

Dialogue Ⅱ:

李 ：<u>すみません</u>。これ、大久保に止まり
str. 5-1 Attracting attention
ますか。

駅員：大久保、ええと、これは快速だから
止まりませんよ。

李 ：<u>止まりません？</u>
str. 1-6 Confirming

駅員：そう、各駅停車に乗って。

李 ：<u>かくえき…？</u>
*str. 1-5 Repeating the part of a word which
you have caught*

駅員：そう。向こうの黄色い電車。

李 ：あ、はい。

Ri: <u>Sumimasen</u>. Kore, Ookubo ni
str. 5-1 Attracting attention
tomarimasu ka.

Ekiin: Ookubo, eeto, kore wa kaisoku da
kara tomarimasen yo.

Ri: <u>Tomarimasen?</u>
str. 1-6 Confirming

Ekiin: Soo, kakueki-teesha ni notte.

Ri: <u>Kakueki…?</u>
*str. 1-5 Repeating the part of a word which you
have caught*

Ekiin: Soo. Mukoo no kiiroi densha.

Ri: A, hai.

8

遊ぶ　Asobu

Going Out

🕶 Dialogues

Ⅰ. Getting information

(Nancy and Mr. Suzuki are looking at an entertainment information magazine.)

ナンシー：鈴木さん、黒沢の映画が見たいんですが。

鈴　木：黒沢の映画ですか。ええと、あっ、新宿で『七人の侍』をやっていますね。

ナンシー：新宿ですね。
str. 2-1, p. 107
新宿のどこですか。

鈴　木：ええと、東映パラス。この地図の11番です。
str. 4-2, p. 107

ナンシー：ああ、ここですか。何時からですか。

鈴　木：ええと、6時半からですね。

Nanshii: Suzuki-san, Kurosawa no eega ga mitai'n desu ga.

Suzuki: Kurosawa no eega desu ka. Eeto, a, Shinjuku de "Shichi-nin no Samurai" o yatte imasu ne.

Nanshii: Shinjuku desu ne.
str. 2-1, p. 107
Shinjuku no doko desu ka.

Suzuki: Eeto, Tooee Parasu. Kono chizu no 11-ban desu.
str. 4-2, p. 107

Nanshii: Aa, koko desu ka. Nan-ji kara desu ka.

Suzuki: Eeto, 6-ji han kara desu ne.

110

Nancy: Mr. Suzuki, I'd like to see a Kurosawa film.

Suzuki: A Kurosawa film? Er, oh, 'Shichi-nin no Samurai' is on in Shinjuku.

Nancy: In Shinjuku. Where is it on in Shinjuku?

Suzuki: Let me see, the Toei Palace. That's No. 11 on this map.

Nancy: Oh, it's here. What time does it start?

Suzuki: Er, from half past six.

黒沢 Kurosawa Kurosawa　映画 eega movie/film　見ます mimasu see　新宿 Shinjuku Shinjuku　やります yarimasu do　地図 chizu map　～番 ～-ban No.～

II. Arranging to go to the movies

ナンシー：あの、鈴木さん。あした暇ですか。

鈴　木：ええ。

ナンシー：じゃ、いっしょに映画を見に行きませんか。

鈴　木：いいですね。

ナンシー：どこで会いましょうか。

鈴　木：6時にアルタの前はどうですか。

ナンシー：えっ、どこですか。
str. 1-5, p. 106

鈴　木．アルタ。新宿駅の近くなんですけど…

ナンシー：じゃ、新宿駅で駅の人に聞きます。

鈴　木：そうですか。

ナンシー：はい。6時ですね。

鈴　木：そうです。

Nanshii: Ano, Suzuki-san. Ashita hima desu ka.

Suzuki: Ee.

Nanshii: Ja, issho ni eega o mi ni ikimasen ka.

Suzuki: Ii desu ne.

Nanshii: Doko de aimashoo ka.

Suzuki: 6-ji ni Aruta no mae wa doo desu ka.

Nanshii: <u>E, doko desu ka.</u>
str. 1-5, p. 106

Suzuki: Aruta. Shinjuku-eki no chikaku na'n desu kedo…

Nanshii: Ja, Shinjuku-eki de eki no hito ni kikimasu.

Suzuki: Soo desu ka.

Nanshii: Hai. 6-ji desu ne.

Suzuki: Soo desu.

111

Nancy: Er, are you free tomorrow, Mr. Suzuki?

Suzuki: Yes, I am.

Nancy: Shall we go and see a film together?

Suzuki: That's a good idea.

Nancy: Where shall we meet?

Suzuki: What do you think of our meeting in front of Alta at six?

Nancy: Where?

Suzuki: In front of Alta. It's near Shinjuku Station.

Nancy: All right, I'll ask someone at the station where it is.

Suzuki: Will you?

Nancy: Yes. At six.

Suzuki: Right.

あした ashita tomorrow　暇[な] hima[na] free　いっしょに issho ni together　行きます ikimasu go　いいですね。 Ii desu ne. That's a good idea.　会います aimasu meet　～はどうですか。 ~ wa doo desu ka. What do you think of ~?　駅 eki station　近く chikaku near　駅の人 eki no hito station employee　聞きます kikimasu ask

III. Talking about films

リ　サ：ナンシーさん、最近おもしろ
　　　　い映画を見ましたか。
ナンシー：はい、きのう黒沢の映画を見
　　　　ました。
リ　サ：そうですか。どうでしたか。
ナンシー：とてもおもしろかったですよ。
　　　　雨のシーンがすごかったです。

Risa:　　Nanshii-san, saikin omoshiroi
　　　　eega o mimashita ka.
Nanshii:　Hai, kinoo Kurosawa no eega o
　　　　mimashita.
Risa:　　Soo desu ka.　Doo deshita ka.
Nanshii:　Totemo omoshirokatta desu yo.
　　　　Ame no shiin ga sugokatta
　　　　desu.

Lisa:　　Have you seen any interesting films
　　　　lately, Nancy?
Nancy:　Yes, I saw a Kurosawa film
　　　　yesterday.
Lisa:　　Did you?　How was it?
Nancy:　I found it very exciting. The rain
　　　　scene was amazing.

112

最近 saikin lately/recently　おもしろい omoshiroi interesting　きのう kinoo yesterday　雨 ame rain　シーン
shiin scene　すごい sugoi amazing/fantastic

 **Grammatical Notes**

1. 〜を見ます。 〜 o mimasu. (Indicating the direct object)

The structure particle **o** is used to connect the verb and the object of a sentence.

Examples: わたしはおもしろい映画を見ました。

Watashi wa omoshiroi eega o mimashita.

I saw an interesting movie.

わたしはＪリーグの試合を見ました。

Watashi wa J-riigu no shiai o mimashita.

I watched a J-league soccer game.

2. 〜ませんか。〜ましょう。 **〜masen ka. 〜mashoo.** (Shall we 〜? Let's 〜)

These expressions are used to invite someone to do something or to ask for someone's company.

Examples: 新宿で映画を見ませんか。

Shinjuku de eega o mimasen ka.

Would you mind going to see a film in Shinjuku with me?

『アラジン』を見に行きませんか。

"Arajin" o mi ni ikimasen ka.

What do you think of seeing *Aladdin* with me?

アルタの前で会いましょう。

Aruta no mae de aimashoo.

Let's meet in front of Alta.

コンサートに行きましょう。

Konsaato ni ikimashoo.

Let's go to a concert.

113

3. The past tense

To make the past tense, verbs and i- and na-adjectives should be conjugated as follows.

verb

Examples: 『アラジン』を見ました。

"Arajin" o mimashita.

I saw *Aladdin*.

わたしは横浜で演劇を見ました。

Watashi wa Yokohama de engeki o mimashita.

I saw a play in Yokohama.

見ます → 見ました
mimasu → mimashita

Ｊリーグ J-riigu J-league 試合 shiai game コンサート konsaato concert 横浜 Yokohama Yokohama 演劇
engeki play

i-adjective

Examples: 『恋愛の法則』はおもしろかったです。

"Ren'ai no hoosoku" wa omoshirokatta desu.

Bodies, Rest & Motion was interesting.

雨のシーンがすごかったです。

Ame no shiin ga sugokatta desu.

The rain scene was amazing.

おもしろいです → おもしろかったです
omoshiroi desu → omoshirokatta desu

na-adjective

Examples: 李さんは暇でした。

Ri-san wa hima deshita.

Ms. Li had ample time to spare.

あの画家の絵はきれいでした。

Ano gaka no e wa kiree deshita.

The paintings of that artist were beautiful.

暇です → 暇でした
hima desu → hima deshita

画家 gaka artist, painter　絵 e picture, painting　きれい［な］kiree[na] beautiful

✎ Exercises

1. Substitution drill: Asking about films

マリオ：李さん、最近（映画）を見まし　　Mario:　Ri-san, saikin (eega) o mimashita ka.
　　　　た。　　　　　　　　　　　　　　Ri:　　Hai, konomae ("Arajin") o mimashita.
　李　：はい、この前（『アラジン』）を見　　　　　　 Sugoku (tanoshikatta) desu.
　　　　ました。すごく（楽しかった）
　　　　です。

例 Ree：映画 eega，　『アラジン』"Arajin"，楽しかった tanoshikatta
　　① 演劇 engeki，　『ミス・サイゴン』"Misu Saigon"，
　　　　つまらなかった tsumaranakatta
　　② スポーツ supootsu，　Ｊリーグの試合 J-riigu no shiai,
　　　　おもしろかった omoshirokatta

2. Substitution drill: Suggesting seeing a film

鈴木：あした、（新宿）で（映画）を見　　Suzuki:　Ashita, (Shinjuku) de (eega) o mimasen
　　　ませんか。　　　　　　　　　　　　　　　　 ka.
アリ：いいですね。見ましょう。　　　　Ari:　　Ii desu ne. Mimashoo.
鈴木：じゃ、7時に駅で会いましょう。　　Suzuki:　Ja, 7-ji ni eki de aimashoo.

例 Ree：新宿 Shinjuku，　映画 eega
　　① 横浜 Yokohama，　演劇 engeki　② 甲子園 Kooshien，　野球 yakyuu

3. Substitution drill: Arranging to meet

鈴木：あした、（横浜）で映画を見ませんか。　Suzuki:　Ashita, (Yokohama) de eega o
アリ：いいですね。どこで会いましょうか。　　　　　 mimasen ka.
鈴木：（6時半）に（高島屋）の前はどう　　Ari:　　Ii desu ne. Doko de aimashoo ka.
　　　ですか。　　　　　　　　　　　　Suzuki:　(6-ji han) ni (Takashimaya) no mae
アリ：（6時半）に（高島屋）の前ですね。　　　　　 wa doo desu ka.
　　　わかりました。　　　　　　　　　Ari:　　(6-ji han) ni (Takashimaya) no mae
　　　　　　　　　　　　　　　　　　　　　　　 desu ne. Wakarimashita.

例 Ree：横浜 Yokohama，　6時半 6-ji han，　高島屋 Takashimaya
　　① 銀座 Ginza，　2時 2-ji，　マリオン Marion
　　② 渋谷 Shibuya，　5時 5-ji，　ハチ公 Hachi-koo
　　③ 池袋 Ikebukuro，　8時20分 8-ji 20-pun，　いけふくろう Ikefukuroo

この前 konomae the other day　楽しい tanoshii delightful　つまらない tsumaranai boring　スポーツ
supootsu sports　甲子園 Kooshien Koshien Stadium　野球 yakyuu baseball　高島屋 Takashimaya
Takashimaya Department Store　わかります wakarimasu understand　銀座 Ginza Ginza　マリオン Marion
Marion　渋谷 Shibuya Shibuya　ハチ公 Hachi-koo Hachi-ko　池袋 Ikebukuro Ikebukuro　いけふくろう
Ikefukuroo Ikefukuro

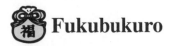 **Fukubukuro**

1. What would you do if...?

Differences between Japanese and English film titles

Read the following dialogue and try to find out solutions to the problems through answering the questions.

ロバート：鈴木さん、最近おもしろい映画を見ましたか。

鈴　木：はい、この前『明日に向かって撃て！』を見ました。

ロバート：『明日に向かって撃て！』ですか。どんな映画ですか。

鈴　木：あれ、知りませんか。有名なアメリカ映画ですけどね。

ロバート：ほんとうですか。

鈴　木：ポール・ニューマンやロバート・レッドフォードが出ているんだけど…

ロバート：それは２人の男の人が追いかけられる西部劇ですか。

鈴　木：そうそう、それです。

ロバート：ああ、*Butch Cassidy and the Sundance Kid* です。

鈴　木：ああ、そういうんですか。

Robert: Have you seen any interesting movies lately, Mr. Suzuki?

Suzuki: Yes, I saw *Shoot Towards Tomorrow!* the other day.

Robert: *Shoot Towards Tomorrow!*? What kind of movie is it?

Suzuki: Oh, don't you know that movie? It's a famous American film.

Robert: Really?

Suzuki: Paul Newman and Robert Redford are in it.

Robert: Is it a cowboy movie about two men being chased?

Suzuki: Yes, yes. That one.

Robert: You mean *Butch Cassidy and the Sundance Kid.*

Suzuki: Really? You call it that?

Questions

(1) Your experience

　・ Have you ever experienced any communication problems when you were talking about films or books?

　・ If your answer to the above question is 'yes,' how did you make yourself understood?

(2) Why do these problems occur?

　・ What prevents you from communicating successfully with Japanese people?

(3) How can these problems be solved?

　・ When Japanese titles of books and films are completely different from the original ones, what can you do for successful communication?

2. Entertainment information

Look at the contents page below and find which page you should turn to when you want to know the following:

(1) the schedule of a concert (clue: コンサート)

(2) information about plays (clue: 演劇)

(3) what films will be on next week (clue: 上映スケジュール)

3. Related words

映画館	eegakan	movie theater
ロードショー	roodo-shoo	first run of a film
上映	jooee	show
洋画	yooga	foreign film
邦画	hooga	Japanese film
俳優	haiyuu	actor/actress
プログラム	puroguramu	program
音楽	ongaku	music
サッカー	sakkaa	soccer
チケット	chiketto	ticket
自由席	jiyuu-seki	non-reserved seat
指定席	shitee-seki	reserved seat
球場	kyuujoo	stadium
情報誌	joohooshi	information magazine
スケジュール	sukejuuru	schedule
日時	nichiji	date and time
料金	ryookin	price
待ち合わせ	machiawase	meeting

Language Focus **Years, Months and Days**

1. Saying Dates

When saying or writing dates in Japanese, you start with the largest figure (the year) and work down to the smallest one (the day).

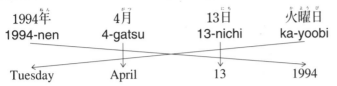

1994年	4月	13日	火曜日
1994-nen	4-gatsu	13-nichi	ka-yoobi

| Tuesday | April | 13 | 1994 |

2. ～年 ～月 ～日 ～曜日 ～-nen ～-gatsu ～-nichi ～-yoobi

The months of the year are numbered. The word for month (-gatsu) is simply attached to the number of the month. Note that the fourth, seventh, and ninth months should be pronounced as shi-gatsu, shichi-gatsu, and ku-gatsu respectively.

To ask what day, month, etc., place nan in front of the relevant time expression.

Examples:
何年	nan-nen	what year
何月	nan-gatsu	what month
何日	nan-nichi	what date
何曜日	nan-yoobi	what day of the week

[handwritten annotations above table: Sun / Moon / Fire / Water / Wood or Tree / gold/Precious Metal / soil Earth]

Sun. 日曜日 nichi-yoobi	Mon. 月曜日 getsu-yoobi	Tue. 火曜日 ka-yoobi	Wed. 水曜日 sui-yoobi	Thu. 木曜日 moku-yoobi	Fri. 金曜日 kin-yoobi	Sat. 土曜日 do-yoobi
1 ついたち tsuitachi	2 ふつか futsuka	3 みっか mikka	4 よっか yokka	5 いつか itsuka	6 むいか muika	7 なのか nanoka
8 ようか yooka	9 ここのか kokonoka	10 とおか tooka	11	12	13	14 じゅうよっか juu yokka
15	16	17	18	19	20 はつか hatsuka	21
22	23	24 にじゅう よっか ni-juu yokka	25	26	27	28
29	30	31				

Note: After 10th, add nichi to all numbers (e.g., juu ichi-nichi) except for 14th, 20th, and 24th.

3. Adverbs of time

おととい	きのう	けさ	きょう	今晩[こんばん]	あした	あさって
ototoi	kinoo	kesa	kyoo	konban	ashita	asatte
the day before yesterday	yesterday	this morning	today	this evening/ tonight	tomorrow	the day after tomorrow

9

飲む　Nomu
Drinking

👀 Dialogues

I. At a Pub/Ordering

店員：いらっしゃいませ。
何名様ですか。
ロバート：2人です。
店員：どうぞこちらへ。

店員：ご注文、お決まりでしょうか。
ロバート：<u>ええと</u>、とりあえずビール
str. 3-1, p. 107
ください。
店員：はい、ビール何本ですか。
ロバート：2本、お願いします。

Ten'in: Irasshaimase. Nan-mee-sama desu ka.
Robaato: Futari desu.
Ten'in: Doozo kochira e.

Ten'in: Go-chuumon, okimari deshoo ka.
Robaato: <u>Eeto</u>, toriaezu biiru kudasai.
str. 3-1, p. 107
Ten'in: Hai, biiru nan-bon desu ka.
Robaato: 2-hon, onegai-shimasu.

Waiter: Welcome. How many people, sir?
Robert: Two.
Waiter: This way, please.

Waiter: Can I take your order?
Robert: Well, beer first.
Waiter: How many, sir?
Robert: Two bottles, please.

いらっしゃいませ。Irasshaimase. Welcome. 何名様 nan-mee-sama how many people <honorific form of nan-nin> 注文 chuumon order お決まりでしょうか。Okimari deshoo ka. May I take your order? とりあえず toriaezu for the moment ビール biiru beer ～本 ～-hon <counter suffix for long things>

II. Discussing what to order

ナンシー：＊ロバートさんは何が好き？
ロバート：焼き鳥。
ナンシー：わたしベジタリアンだから、肉はだめなんです。
ロバート：えっ、そう？　野菜しか食べないの？
ナンシー：そう。わたし卵サラダにする。
ロバート：ああ、ぼくはアレルギーがあるから、卵は食べられないんだよ。
ナンシー：そう？
ロバート：うん。だから、ワカメサラダにするよ。注文しよう。

Nanshii: ＊Robaato-san wa nani ga suki?
Robaato: Yakitori.
Nanshii: Watashi bejitarian da kara, niku wa damena'n desu.
Robaato: E, soo?　Yasai shika tabenai no?
Nanshii: Soo. Watashi tamago-sarada ni suru.
Robaato: Aa, boku wa arerugii ga aru kara, tamago wa taberarenai'n da yo.
Nanshii: Soo?
Robaato: Un. Dakara, wakame-sarada ni suru yo. Chuumon-shiyoo.

Nancy: What would you like, Robert?
Robert: Yakitori.
Nancy: I'm a vegetarian, so I don't eat meat.
Robert: Really? You only eat vegetables?
Nancy: That's right. So I'll order salad with eggs.
Robert: Oh, I have an allergy to eggs.
Nancy: Is that so?
Robert: Yeah. So I'll have a seaweed salad. Let's order.

＊ At this point, Nancy and Robert start talking in an informal way.

好き［な］ suki[na] like 焼き鳥 yakitori yakitori ベジタリアン bejitarian vegetarian 肉 niku meat だめです dame desu not O.K./unacceptable 野菜 yasai vegetable 食べます tabemasu eat 卵 tamago egg サラダ sarada salad ～にします ～ ni shimasu I'll have ～ アレルギー arerugii allergy だから dakara so ワカメ wakame seaweed 注文します chuumon-shimasu order

 **Grammatical Notes**

1. 〜本 〜-hon (Counter suffix for long things)

The counter suffix -hon is used to count long things such as pencils and bottles. Depending on the preceding number, it may be pronounced either -hon, -bon, or -pon.

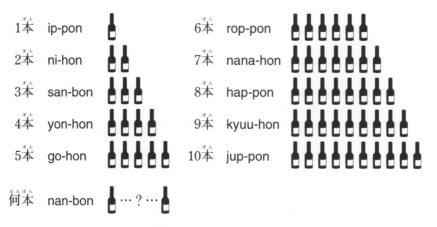

1本	ip-pon		6本	rop-pon
2本	ni-hon		7本	nana-hon
3本	san-bon		8本	hap-pon
4本	yon-hon		9本	kyuu-hon
5本	go-hon		10本	jup-pon
何本	nan-bon			

2. 〜が好きです。 〜 ga suki desu. (like 〜)

This sentence pattern is used to say what you are fond of. Pay attention to the structure particle ga. Desu is used only in formal style sentences; it is not used in informal ones.

Examples: ビールが好きです。
Biiru ga suki desu.
I like beer.

お酒が好きです。
O-sake ga suki desu.
I like sake.

3. 〜はだめです。 〜 wa dame desu. (don't eat/drink 〜)

This pattern is used to say what you can't/don't eat or drink. Attention should be paid to the particle wa.

Examples: 豚肉はだめです。
Butaniku wa dame desu.
I can't eat pork.

肉はだめです。
Niku wa dame desu.
I don't eat meat.

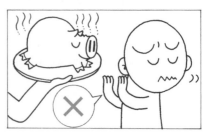

（お）酒 (o-) sake sake　豚肉 butaniku pork

4. Dictionary form of verbs

Examples: わたし卵サラダにする。

      Watashi tamago-sarada ni suru.

      I'll have salad with eggs.

      ぼくはアレルギーがある。

      Boku wa arerugii ga aru.

      I have an allergy.

The words in red type are verbs in the dictionary form. The way of making the dictionary form from the **masu**-form of a verb depends on the verb group. The table below shows how to make the dictionary form for each verb group.

	ます形	辞書形
I	書き（ます）	書く
	急ぎ	急ぐ
	飲み	飲む
	呼び	呼ぶ
	取り	取る
	買い	買う
	待ち	待つ
	話し	話す
II	食べ	食べる
	換え	換える
	起き	起きる
III	来	来る
	し	する

	masu-form	dictionary-form
I	kaki(masu)	kaku
	isogi	isogu
	nomi	nomu
	yobi	yobu
	tori	toru
	kai	kau
	machi	matsu
	hanashi	hanasu
II	tabe	taberu
	kae	kaeru
	oki	okiru
III	ki	kuru
	shi	suru

125

5. ～んです。 ～ 'n desu. (Explaining the current situation)

This is an expression used to explain the current situation in order to obtain the listener's understanding.

Example: わたしはベジタリアンだから、肉はだめなんです。

      Watashi wa bejitarian da kara, niku wa damena'n desu.

      I am a vegetarian, so I don't eat meat.

If you simply say, Niku wa dame desu, it is too blunt and sounds as if you don't care whether you are understood or not.

    This expression is used with the plain forms of verbs, i-adjectives, na-adjectives, and nouns. (For plain forms, see page 130, where you will find a table that compares polite and plain forms.) In the example above, however, there is an anomaly:

    dame da + 'n desu → damena'n desu

✏️ Exercises

1. Change the following verbs into their dictionary forms.

例 Ree：卵サラダにします tamago-sarada ni shimasu
→ 卵サラダにする tamago-sarada ni suru

(1) アレルギーがあります arerugii ga arimasu →

(2) 焼き鳥を注文します yakitori o chuumon-shimasu →

(3) 野菜を食べます yasai o tabemasu →

2. State what you like in the picture below.

A：あなたは何が好きですか。　　　A: Anata wa nani ga suki desu ka.

B：（　　　　　　　）が好きです。　B: (　　　　　　) ga suki desu.

3. Substitution drill: Saying numbers of bottles

店　員：ビール何本ですか。　　　Ten'in: Biiru nan-bon desu ka.

マリオ：（2）本、お願いします。　Mario: (2)-hon, onegai-shimasu.

例 Ree：🍶🍶　①🍶　②🍶🍶🍶　③🍶🍶🍶🍶🍶

4. Substitution drill: Talking about food that you cannot eat

A：（オムレツ）はどうですか。　　A: (Omuretsu) wa doo desu ka.

B：わたし、（卵）はだめなんです。　B: Watashi, (tamago) wa damena'n desu.

A：えっ、どうしてですか。　　　　A: E, dooshite desu ka.

B：（卵アレルギーなんです。）　　B: (Tamago-arerugii na'n desu.)

例 Ree：オムレツ omuretsu, 卵 tamago, 卵アレルギーなんです。Tamago-arerugii na'n desu.

① 焼き鳥 yakitori, 肉 niku, ベジタリアンなんです。 Bejitarian na'n desu.

② アスパラのベーコン巻 asupara no beekon-maki, 豚肉 butaniku,
イスラム教徒なんです。 Isuramu-kyooto na'n desu.

③ 刺身の盛り合わせ sashimi no moriawase, 刺身 sashimi,
生の魚はちょっと。 Nama no sakana wa chotto.

オムレツ omuretsu omelette　アスパラのベーコン巻 asupara no beekon-maki asparagus and bacon roll　イスラム教徒 Isuramu-kyooto Muslim　刺身 sashimi sashimi　盛り合わせ moriawase selection　生 nama raw
魚 sakana fish　〜はちょっと。 ～ wa chotto. <used to refuse things in an indirect, polite way>

 **Fukubukuro**

1. What would you do if...?

Asked to go out drinking

Read the following dialogue and try to find out solutions to the problems through answering the questions.

林　：池田さん、今晩どう？　野球部の忘年会。

池田：ええっ、きのうも忘年会だったし、きょう
　　　は勘弁してくださいよ。あしたは９時から
　　　会議がありますから。

林　：何言ってんだよ。年末だよ、年末。パッと
　　　行こうぜ。

池田：林さん、忘年会いくつ出てるんですか。

林　：さあ、いくつかな…

池田：ほんとにもう。ゆうべはあれからどうした
　　　んですか。

林　：あれから３軒ははしごしたよ。今晩、一次会
　　　だけならつきあえるだろ？

池田：林さんは強いからいいけど、…

林　：ま、そう言わずに行こう、行こう。

Hayashi: Mr. Ikeda, how about (going out for a drink) tonight? It's the baseball team's 'bonenkai (year-end party).'

Ikeda: Oh no! We had a 'bonenkai' last night, too. Please let me off tonight. Tomorrow I have to attend a meeting from nine o'clock.

Hayashi: What are you saying? It's the end of the year. Let's paint the town red.

Ikeda: How many 'bonenkai' have you been to (this year)?

Hayashi: Well, I'm not sure...

Ikeda: You're unbelievable. What did you do last night after I left?

Hayashi: We went to three more bars. Tonight, just come to one place.

Ikeda: You can take a lot of drink, Mr. Hayashi, but I...

Hayashi: Don't say that. Let's go. Let's go.

Questions

(1) Your experience
　· Do you drink every evening?
　· Are there people around you who drink every night? What do you think of those people?
　· Have you ever been repeatedly asked to go out drinking when you didn't want to go? How did you feel at that time?

(2) Why does this kind of thing happen?
　· Why do such people not consider other people's feelings or schedules?

(3) How can such difficulties be solved?
　· When asking someone to go drinking, what should you consider?
　· If you were repeatedly asked to go drinking, what would you do?

2. Useful words

例 Ree：酒	① piza	a. fried potato
(1)ワカメサラダ	② uisukii	b. croquette
(2)フライド・ポテト	③ biiru	c. pizza
(3)コロッケ	④ furaido-poteto	d. whisky
(4)チーズ	⑤ nikujaga	e. beer
(5)ピザ	⑥ wakame-sarada	f. cheese
(6)ビール	⑦ chiizu	g. sake
(7)肉じゃが	⑧ tori no karaage	h. seaweed salad
(8)ウイスキー	⑨ korokke	i. yen
(9)鳥の唐揚げ	⑩ sake	j. beef and potato stew
(10)円	⑪ en	k. fried chicken

3. Related words

飲み屋	nomiya	pub	チーズ	chiizu	cheese
居酒屋	izakaya	bar	コロッケ	korokke	croquette
バー	baa	snack bar	ピザ	piza	pizza
日本酒	Nihonshu	Japanese sake	冷ややっこ	hiyayakko	cold tofu
ウイスキー	uisukii	whisky	板わさ	itawasa	sliced fish paste
水割り	mizuwari	(whisky) with water	てんぷら	tenpura	tempura (deep-fried fish and vegetables)
ワイン	wain	wine			
カクテル	kakuteru	cocktail	ソーセージ	sooseeji	sausage
ジュース	juusu	juice	～個	～-ko	<counter suffix for small things>
コカ・コーラ	koka-koora	Coca Cola			
おつまみ	otsumami	bar snack	～枚	～-mai	<counter suffix for flat things>
フライド・ポテト	furaido-poteto	fried potato	～杯	～-hai	<counter suffix for drinks>
肉じゃが	nikujaga	beef and potato stew	相席	aiseki	sharing a table
鳥の唐揚げ	tori no karaage	fried chicken	メニュー	menyuu	menu
枝豆	edamame	green soybeans	お勘定	o-kanjoo	bill

Language Focus **Polite and Plain Styles**

Compare the following two conversations.

女：森田さん、おはようございます。
男：ああ、おはようございます。
女：あした、暇ですか。
男：はい。
女：じゃ、新宿で映画を見ませんか。
男：いいですね。どこで会いましょうか。
女：7時にアルタの前はどうですか。
男：7時にアルタの前ですね。
　　わかりました。
女：じゃ、またあした。

女：森田君、おはよう。
男：ああ、おはよう。
女：あした暇？
男：うん。
女：じゃ、新宿で映画見ない？
男：ああ、いいね。どこで会おうか。
女：7時にアルタの前はどう？
男：7時にアルタの前だね。
　　うん、わかった。
女：じゃ、あしたね。

Onna:　Morita-san, ohayoo gozaimasu.
Otoko: Aa, ohayoo gozaimasu.
Onna:　Ashita, hima desu ka.
Otoko: Hai.
Onna:　Ja, Shinjuku de eega o mimasen ka.
Otoko: Ii desu ne. Doko de aimashoo ka.
Onna:　7-ji ni Aruta no mae wa doo desu ka.
Otoko: 7-ji ni Aruta no mae desu ne.
　　　　Wakarimashita.
Onna:　Ja, mata ashita.

Onna:　Morita-kun, ohayoo.
Otoko: Aa, ohayoo.
Onna:　Ashita hima?
Otoko: Un.
Onna:　Ja, Shinjuku de eega minai?
Otoko: Aa, ii ne. Doko de aoo ka.
Onna:　7-ji ni Aruta no mae wa doo?
Otoko: 7-ji ni Aruta no mae da ne.
　　　　Un, wakatta.
Onna:　Ja, ashita ne.

129

Woman: Good morning, Mr. Morita.
Man:　　Oh, good morning.
Woman: Are you free tomorrow?
Man:　　Yes.
Woman: What do you think of going to see a film in Shinjuku?
Man:　　Good idea. Where shall we meet?
Woman: How about in front of Alta at seven?
Man:　　In front of Alta at seven. O.K.
Woman: See you tomorrow.

Woman: Morning, Yutaka.
Man:　　Oh, morning.
Woman: Are you free tomorrow?
Man:　　Yes.
Woman: Do you fancy seeing a film in Shinjuku?
Man:　　Yes, alright. Where do you want to meet?
Woman: In front of Alta at seven?
Man:　　In front of Alta at seven. O.K.
Woman: See you tomorrow.

The two in the left-hand side conversation are not strangers, but it is not very long since they first met each other. Their conversation therefore sounds rather formal. The other couple on the other hand are speaking in an informal manner as they are classmates and very friendly with each other. Note that kun is not normally used in work situations. The language used in formal and informal situations is differentiated as explained on the next page.

1. Polite and Plain Styles

The subject matter of the conversations on the previous page is more or less the same, but the conversational styles are quite different. The conversation on the left side is polite in style, while the one on the right side is plain. In Japanese, language is divided between polite and plain styles, and the type you use depends on the situation and the person you are talking to. The word at the end of the sentence will dictate its level of politeness. Each part of speech has a polite and a plain form.

		polite form		plain form	
		affirmative	negative	affirmative	negative
verb	non-past	見ます mimasu	見ません mimasen	見る miru	見ない minai
	past	見ました mimashita	見ませんでした mimasendeshita	見た mita	見なかった minakatta
i-adjective	non-past	いいです ii desu	よくないです yokunai desu	いい ii	よくない yokunai
	past	よかったです yokatta desu	よくなかったです yokunakatta desu	よかった yokatta	よくなかった yokunakatta
na-adjective	non-past	暇です hima desu	暇ではありません hima dewa arimasen	暇だ hima da	暇ではない hima dewa nai
	past	暇でした hima deshita	暇ではありませんでした hima dewa arimasendeshita	暇だった hima datta	暇ではなかった hima dewa nakatta
noun	non-past	前です mae desu	前ではありません mae dewa arimasen	前だ mae da	前ではない mae dewa nai
	past	前でした mae deshita	前ではありませんでした mae dewa arimasendeshita	前だった mae datta	前ではなかった mae dewa nakatta

Which type of language should be used in the following situations, polite or plain? Encircle the right one. (Correct answers are given on page 190.)

1. You are introducing yourself to someone for the first time.

   Polite   Plain

2. You are attending a meeting with your boss.

   Polite   Plain

3. You are making holiday plans with your friends.

   Polite   Plain

4. You are receiving instructions or directions from your manager.

   Polite   Plain

5. You are chatting with your colleagues during a lunch break.

   Polite   Plain

2. Greetings and Set Phrases

There are formal and informal ways of saying certain greetings and set phrases. (See those expressions underlined twice in the conversation on p. 129.) See **Greeting and Set Phrases** on pp. 40-43.

10

銀行　Ginkoo
（ぎんこう）

Banks

👀 Dialogues

Ⅰ. At the entrance of a bank/Locating the right window

銀行員：いらっしゃいませ。

ア　リ：<u>すみません</u>。
　　　　str. 5-1, p. 107
　　　　お金を換えたいんですが。

銀行員：外貨ですか。

ア　リ：はい、ドルを円に換えたいん
　　　　ですが。

銀行員：＊では、お２階になりますので、
　　　　あちらからお上がりください。

Ginkooin: Irasshaimase.

Ari:　　 <u>Sumimasen</u>.
　　　　 str. 5-1, p. 107
　　　　 O-kane o kaetai'n desu ga.

Ginkooin: Gaika desu ka.

Ari:　　 Hai, doru o en ni kaetai'n
　　　　 desu ga.

Ginkooin: ＊Dewa, o-2-kai ni narimasu
　　　　　 node, achira kara o-agari
　　　　　 kudasai.

Clerk: Welcome.

Ali:　 Excuse me. I would like to exchange
　　　 money.

Clerk: Exchange foreign currency?

Ali:　 Yes, I would like to exchange dollars
　　　 for yen.

Clerk: The foreign exchange section is on
　　　 the second floor. Please use the stairs
　　　 over there.

＊People who deal with customers use polite expressions.

お金 o-kane money　換えます kaemasu exchange　外貨 gaika foreign currency　ドル doru dollar　円 en yen
（お）２階 (o-)2-kai the second floor　〜になります 〜ni narimasu <used in place of desu by people dealing
with customers>　あちら achira over there　上がります agarimasu go upstairs

Ⅱ. At the foreign exchange window/Exchanging foreign currency

アリ：すみません。
　　　ドルを円に換えたいんですが。

銀行員：はい。いくらですか。

アリ：100ドルです。

銀行員：現金ですか。

アリ：はい。

銀行員：では、こちらの用紙に記入してください。*(She hands over a form.)*

アリ：すみません。何を書けばいいんですか。

銀行員：こちらに金額とお名前を書いてください。

アリ：<u>はい。</u>
　　　str. 2-2, p. 107

銀行員：そしてご住所と電話番号です。

アリ：はい、わかりました。

Ari:　　　Sumimasen.
　　　　　Doru o en ni kaetai'n desu ga.

Ginkooin: Hai. Ikura desu ka.

Ari:　　　100-doru desu.

Ginkooin: Genkin desu ka.

Ari:　　　Hai.

Ginkooin: Dewa, kochira no yooshi ni kinyuu-shite kudasai.
　　　　　(She hands over a form.)

Ari:　　　Sumimasen. Nani o kakeba ii'n desu ka.

Ginkooin: Kochira ni kingaku to o-namae o kaite kudasai.

Ari:　　　<u>Hai.</u>
　　　　　str. 2-2, p. 107

Ginkooin: Soshite go-juusho to denwa-bangoo desu.

Ari:　　　Hai, wakarimashita.

135

Ali:　 Excuse me. I would like to exchange dollars for yen.

Clerk: How much?

Ali:　 100 dollars.

Clerk: Cash?

Ali:　 Yes.

Clerk: Would you fill in this form, please?
　　　(She hands over a form.)

Ali:　 Sorry, what should I write here?

Clerk: Write the dollar amount and your name here.

Ali:　 All right.

Clerk: And then your address and telephone number.

Ali:　 I see.

いくら ikura how much　現金 genkin cash　用紙 yooshi form　記入します kinyuu-shimasu fill in, write　書きます kakimasu write　金額 kingaku amount　（お）名前 (o-)namae name　（ご）住所 (go-)juusho address　電話番号 denwa-bangoo telephone number

Ⅲ. At a cash dispenser/Checking opening times

(Robert is at a bank. It's 3:30 p.m. now. Only the cash dispenser area is open, and there are no bank clerks around. He speaks to a customer at the cash dispenser.)

ロバート：すみません。お金を換えたいんですが、どこに行けばいいですか。

ほかの客：えっと、ドルですか。

ロバート：はい。

ほかの客：もう銀行は閉まってますから、きょうはできないと思います。

ロバート：<u>えっ、閉まってます？</u>
str. 1-5, p. 106

ほかの客：ええ。

ロバート：ああ、そうですか。何時までなんですか。

ほかの客：3時までです。

Robaato:　Sumimasen.
　　　　　O-kane o kaetai'n desu ga, doko ni ikeba ii desu ka.

Hoka no kyaku: Etto, doru desu ka.

Robaato:　Hai.

Hoka no kyaku: Moo ginkoo wa shimatte masu kara, kyoo wa dekinai to omoimasu.

Robaato:　<u>E, shimatte masu?</u>
　　　　　str. 1-5, p. 106

Hoka no kyaku: Ee.

Robaato:　Aa, soo desu ka. Nan-ji made na'n desu ka.

Hoka no kyaku: 3-ji made desu.

136

Robert: Excuse me. Where can I exchange money?

Man:　You mean dollars?

Robert: Yes.

Man:　The bank has closed for today. I am afraid you can't do it today.

Robert: Closed?

Man:　Yes.

Robert: I see. What time does it close?

Man:　At three.

もう moo already　銀行 ginkoo bank　閉まります shimarimasu close　きょう kyoo today　できます dekimasu can do　何時まで nan-ji made until what time

Grammatical Notes

1. ～たいんですが。 ～tai'n desu ga. (I would like to ～.)

This expression is used to tell people what you want to do.

Examples: ドルを換えたいんですが。
Doru o kaetai'n desu ga.
I would like to exchange dollars.

お金を送りたいんですが。
O-kane o okuritai'n desu ga.
I would like to make a remittance.

The underlined verbs in the above examples are in the masu-form. This sentence pattern consists of the masu-form of a verb + tai'n desu ga.

2. ～てください。 ～te kudasai. (Would you ～?)

This expression is used to make requests and to ask for assistance.

Examples: 円に換えてください。   少し待ってください。
En ni kaete kudasai.   Sukoshi matte kudasai.
Would you exchange this for yen?   Would you wait for a moment?

The underlined verbs in the above examples are in the te-form. This sentence pattern consists of the te-form of a verb + kudasai. The way of making the te-form from the masu-form depends on the verb group. The table below shows how to make the te-form from the masu-form of each verb group.

	ます形	て形
I	書き(ます)	書いて
	急ぎ	急いで
	飲み	飲んで
	呼び	呼んで
	取り	取って
	買い	買って
	待ち	待って
	話し	話して
II	食べ	食べて
	換え	換えて
	起き	起きて
III	来	来て
	し	して

	masu-form	te-form
I	kaki(masu)	kaite
	isogi	isoide
	nomi	nonde
	yobi	yonde
	tori	totte
	kai	katte
	machi	matte
	hanashi	hanashite
II	tabe	tabete
	kae	kaete
	oki	okite
III	ki	kite
	shi	shite

* The te-form of ikimasu is not iite but itte.

送ります okurimasu remit   少し sukoshi a little   待ちます machimasu wait

✐ Exercises

1. **What is the bank clerk saying in each picture? Choose the appropriate answer from (a), (b), (c) and (d).**

(1) (   )   (2) (   )   (3) (   )   (4) (   )

(a) こちらの用紙に記入してください。　　Kochira no yooshi ni kinyuu-shite kudasai.
(b) あちらで少し待ってください。　　　　Achira de sukoshi matte kudasai.
(c) 確かめてください。　　　　　　　　　Tashikamete kudasai.
(d) 2階へ行ってください。　　　　　　　2-kai e itte kudasai.

2. **Substitution drill: Making requests**

ロバート：すみませんが、ちょっと　　　　Robaato: Sumimasen ga, chotto (oshiete)
　　　　　（教えて）ください。　　　　　　　　　kudasai.
銀行員：はい。　　　　　　　　　　　　Ginkooin: Hai.

例 Ree：教えて oshiete　① 書いて kaite　② 待って matte

3. **Substitution drill: Sending money**

客　：すみません。（ペルー）へお金を　Kyaku:　Sumimasen. (Peruu) e o-kane o
　　　送りたいんですが。　　　　　　　　　　　okuritai'n desu ga.
銀行員：はい。いくら送りますか。　　　Ginkooin: Hai. Ikura okurimasu ka.
客　：（30,000円）です。　　　　　　Kyaku:　(30,000-en) desu.

例 Ree：ペルー Peruu, 30,000円 30,000-en
① アメリカ Amerika, 100ドル 100-doru
② 中国 Chuugoku, 10,000円 10,000-en
③ フィリピン Firipin, 30ドル 30-doru

138

確かめます tashikamemasu confirm　ちょっと chotto a little　教えます oshiemasu tell　ペルー Peruu Peru
中国 Chuugoku China　フィリピン Firipin the Philippines

1. Extended activities

(1) How to fill in an overseas remittance form

This is the form to be used in requesting remittance through a bank. Try to fill in the form now, assuming that you are now making remittance to your friend. Write in block alphabetical letters.

送金種類 (REMITTANCE BY)	☐ 電信送金 (TELEGRAPHIC TRANSFER) ☐ 普通送金 (MAIL TRANSFER) ☐ 送金小切手 (DEMAND DRAFT)	帳票区分	
	☐ 通知払 (ADVISE & PAY) ☐ 当座口振込 (ADVISE & CREDIT) ☐ 請求払 (PAY ON DEMAND)	反復契約番号 /FB受付番号	取組日 (DATE)
通貨種類 (KIND OF CURRENCY)	送金金額 (AMOUNT OF REMITTANCE)	→EQUIVALENT TO（異種通貨による送金の場合、原通貨金額をご記入下さい。） ←通貨(CURRENCY)　金額(AMOUNT)	
ご依頼人名 (APPLICANT) 住所 (ADDRESS) 電話番号 (TEL)		ご依頼人貨外口座番号(当行記入欄)　お客様摘要番号 (APPLICANT REF. NO.) ご依頼人署名または記名捺印 (SIGNATURE)	
仕向銀行 (PAYING BANK)		コルレスコード　送金目的および許可番号 (PURPOSE & LICENSE NO.)	
受取人 (BENEFICIARY)	支払銀行 (BENEFICIARY'S ACCOUNT WITH BANK) 口座番号 (A/C NO.) 氏名 (NAME) 住所 (ADDRESS)	コルレスコード 商品コード 国名(COUNTRY) 特に受取人あて連絡すべき事項があればご記入下さい。(スペースを含み140字以内。) (MESSAGE TO PAYEE IF ANY.)	
支払銀行手数料 (CHARGES DUE TO PAYING BANK TO BE BORNE BY)	☐ 受取人負担(BENEFICIARY) ☐ 依頼人負担(APPLICANT) 上記になんら指示がない場合は受取人負担としてください。(BENEFICIARY'S A/C UNLESS INSTRUCTED ABOVE.)	手数料負担区分依頼人の場合 支払銀行手数料徴収区分	前取り	後取り
代り金決済方法	☐外貨払 ☐円貨払(SPOT) ☐異種通貨払(C/O)(SPOT) 　　　 ☐円貨払(CONT) ☐異種通貨払(C/O)(CONT) 先物取引明細 (FORWARD EXCHANGE TRANSACTION) 番号 SFB　レート ¥ 　　　　　　　　番番 CFB　レート ・	送金代り金を口座より引落しされる方のみご記入下さい。(口座張替依頼書御届出済の場合ご記入不要です。) ☐ 普通預金 (届出印鑑もしくは署名) ☐ 当座預金 ☐ 口座番号 （　　　　　）	

（太線の中のみご記入下さい。なお☐欄には該当箇所に×印を付けてください。 FILL IN THE THE THICK LINED SPACE ONLY MARK WITH "X" NECESSARY COLUMNS）

139

(2) Business hours and closed days

Check the closed days and business hours of Japanese banks and cash machines.

2. Useful words

Which window is the right one in the following cases?

(1) When you want to exchange 100 dollars for yen. (   )

(2) When you want to send 6,000 yen to your country. (   )

(3) When you want to deposit 5,000 yen. (   )

① お預け入れ　② お引き出し　③ ご相談　④ 外国為替

3. Related words

銀行員	ginkooin	bank clerk
預金	yokin	savings/deposit
口座	kooza	account
印鑑	inkan	seal/stamp
下ろします	oroshimasu	withdraw
送金します	sookin-shimasu	send money
通帳	tsuuchoo	bankbook
預け入れ	azukeire	deposit
引き出し	hikidashi	withdrawal
振り込み	furikomi	transfer/paying in
ご相談	go-soodan	consultation
外国為替	gaikoku-kawase	foreign exchange
トラベラーズ・チェック	toraberaazu-chekku	traveler's check

140

Summary of Interrogative Words

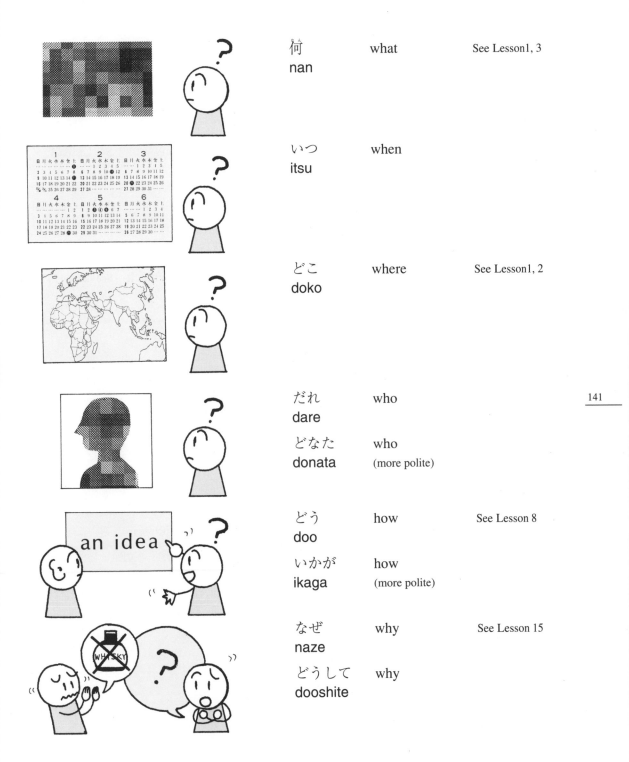

何 nan	what	See Lesson 1, 3
いつ itsu	when	
どこ doko	where	See Lesson 1, 2
だれ dare	who	
どなた donata	who (more polite)	
どう doo	how	See Lesson 8
いかが ikaga	how (more polite)	
なぜ naze	why	See Lesson 15
どうして dooshite	why	

an idea

141

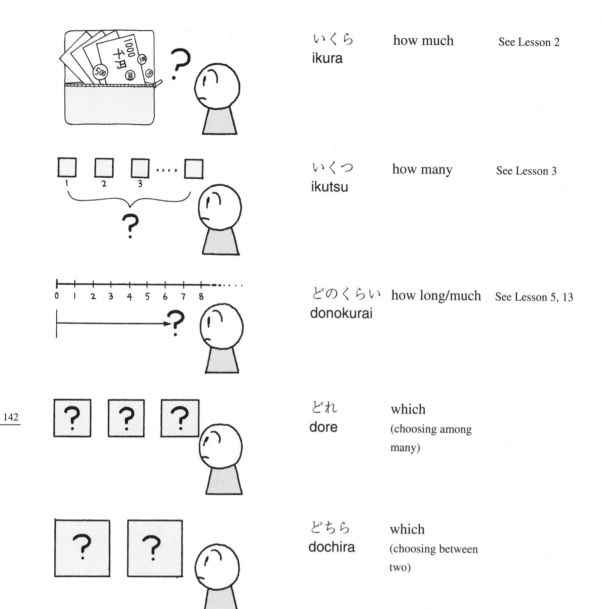

いくら　　　　how much　　　See Lesson 2
ikura

いくつ　　　　how many　　　See Lesson 3
ikutsu

どのくらい　how long/much　See Lesson 5, 13
donokurai

どれ　　　　which
dore　　　　(choosing among many)

どちら　　　which
dochira　　(choosing between two)

11

働く　Hataraku

Working

👀 Dialogues

Ⅰ. At work/Asking to have lunch with someone

マリオ：田中さん、いっしょに食べて
　　　　もいいですか。

田　中：ああ、どうぞ。

- -

マリオ：田中さん、
　　　　それは何て言うんですか。
　　　　str. 3-2, p. 107

田　中：これは「弁当」。

マリオ：ああ、べんとう。おいしいですか。
　　　　str. 2-1, p. 107

田　中：うん、おいしいよ。

Mario:　Can I have lunch with you, Mr.
　　　　Tanaka?

Tanaka: Oh, sure.

- -

Mario:　Mr. Tanaka, what is that called?

Tanaka: This is called a 'bento (box lunch).'

Mario:　'Bento.' Is it good?

Tanaka: Yes, it is.

Mario:　Tanaka-san, issho ni tabete mo
　　　　ii desu ka.

Tanaka: Aa, doozo.

- -

Mario:　Tanaka-san,
　　　　<u>sore wa nan te iu'n desu ka.</u>
　　　　str. 3-2, p. 107

Tanaka: Kore wa 'bentoo'.

Mario:　Aa, <u>bentoo</u>. Oishii desu ka.
　　　　str. 2-1, p. 107

Tanaka: Un, oishii yo.

144

いっしょに issho ni together 食べます tabemasu eat どうぞ。 Doozo. Please. それ sore that 〜は何て言
うんですか。 〜 wa nan te iu'n desu ka. What do you call 〜? これ kore this 弁当 bentoo box lunch おい
しい oishii delicious

II. At work/Asking to borrow something

田中：マリオさん、このワープロ、
　　　ちょっと借りてもいい [ですか]？

マリオ：はい、どうぞ。

マリオ：ううん、ちょっと…
　　　　今から、使いたいんですが…
田中：ああ、そう[ですか]。じゃ、あとで。
マリオ：はい。

Tanaka: Mario-san, kono waapuro,
　　　　chotto karite mo ii [desu ka]?

Mario:　Hai, doozo.

Mario:　Uun, chotto…
　　　　Ima kara, tsukaitai'n desu ga…
Tanaka: Aa, soo [desu ka]. Ja, ato de.
Mario:　Hai.

Tanaka:　Can I borrow this word processor, Mario?

Mario:　Sure.

Mario:　Well, I... I would like to use it now.
Tanaka: I see. Later, then.
Mario:　All right.

145

Note: Without the words in brackets, the conversation is much more informal in style.

この kono this ～ ワープロ waapuro word processor 借ります karimasu borrow 今から ima kara from now あとで ato de later

Ⅲ. In a factory/Asking if one can smoke

マリオ：田中さん、たばこを
　　　　吸ってもいいですか。

禁煙

田中：ああ、いい［です］よ。

田　中：ここは、だめだめ。
　　　　あそこで、吸って［ください］。
マリオ：はい、あの、あれは何て読むんですか。
　　　　str. 1-7, p. 106
田　中：えっ、ああ、あれは「きんえん」
　　　　［です］。
マリオ：きんえん？ No smoking?
　　　　str. 2-1, p. 107　*str. 3-5, p. 107*
田　中：そう。

Mario: Tanaka-san, tabako o
　　　　sutte mo ii desu ka.

Tanaka: Aa, ii [desu] yo.

Tanaka: Koko wa, dame dame.
　　　　Asoko de, sutte [kudasai].
Mario:　Hai, ano, are wa nan te yomu'n desu ka.
　　　　str. 1-7, p. 106
Tanaka: E, aa, are wa 'kin'en' [desu].
Mario:　Kin'en?　　'No smoking'?
　　　　str. 2-1, p. 107　*str. 3-5, p. 107*
Tanaka: Soo.

Mario:　May I smoke, Mr. Tanaka?

Tanaka: Sure.

Tanaka: No, not here.
　　　　You should smoke over there.
Mario:　How do you read that?
Tanaka: That one? It reads 'kin'en.'
Mario:　'Kin'en'? No smoking?
Tanaka: That's right.

Note: Without the words in brackets, the conversation is much more informal in style.

たばこ tabako cigarette　吸います suimasu smoke　ここ koko here　だめ dame not O.K.　あそこ asoko over there　何て読むんですか。Nan te yomu'n desu ka. How do you read that?　禁煙 kin'en no smoking

 **Grammatical Notes**

1. ～てもいいですか。～**te mo ii desu ka.** (Asking for permission)

If you do not know the te-form, read page 137.

写真を撮ります shashin o torimasu（Ⅰ） You want to take photos.	とって totte
食べます tabemasu（Ⅱ） You want to eat something.	たべて tabete
見学します kengaku-shimasu（Ⅲ） You want to go on a field trip.	けんがくして kengaku-shite
たばこを吸います tabako o suimasu（Ⅰ） You want to smoke.	すって sutte
借ります karimasu（Ⅱ） You want to borrow something.	かりて karite
使います tsukaimasu（Ⅰ） You want to use something.	つかって tsukatte
休みます yasumimasu（Ⅰ） You want to take a rest.	やすんで yasunde
トイレへ行きます toire e ikimasu（Ⅰ） You want to go to the bathroom.	いって itte
帰ります kaerimasu（Ⅰ） You want to leave work early.	かえって kaette

When do you have to get permission in your daily life?
Using the example situations below, ask for permission.

もいいですか。
mo ii desu ka.

↓

How to use in practice:

あのう、 | 写真を撮って | もいいですか。
Anoo, | shashin o totte | mo ii desu ka.

Excuse me, may I take photos?

Note:（Ⅰ）（Ⅱ）（Ⅲ）indicate the verb group.

147

2. どうぞ／ちょっと／だめです。 **doozo／chotto／dame desu**
   (Giving/refusing permission)

はい、どうぞ。	Hai, doozo.	Sure.
ちょっと…	Chotto…	Well, I...
いいえ、だめです。	Iie, dame desu.	No, you may not.

Chotto is used when you are declining someone's request for personal reasons. Dame desu is used when someone's request is rejected because of regulations or rules.

3. ～は何て言う/読むんですか。 **～ wa nan te iu/yomu'n desu ka.**
   (How do you say/read ～ ?)

The above expressions can be used when you want to know the pronunciation or reading of a character.

これは何て言うんですか。—「弁当」です。
Kore wa nan te iu'n desu ka. —'Bentoo' desu.
What do you call this? —That's a 'bento.'

あれは何て読むんですか。—「禁煙」です。
Are wa nan te yomu'n desu ka. —'Kin'en' desu.
How do you read that? —'Kin'en.'

✎ Exercises

1. Substitution drill: Asking for permission

Speaking to your colleague →

( ) さん、( )-san,

Asking for permission →

いっしょに（食べて）もいいですか。 Issho ni (tabete) mo ii desu ka.

Giving permission →

ああ、どうぞ。Aa, doozo.

例 Ree : 食べて tabete

① 飲んで nonde　② 見て mite　③ 写真を撮って shashin o totte

2. Using the following dialogue as an example, try to borrow the things listed below.

Attracting attention →

( ) さん、この（はさみ） ( )-san, kono (hasami)

Asking for permission →

ちょっと、借りてもいいですか。 chotto, karite mo ii desu ka.

Giving permission →

はい、どうぞ。Hai, doozo.

Refusing permission →

ううん、ちょっと。Uun, chotto.

Showing gratitude or understanding →

どうも。Doomo.

例 Ree : はさみ hasami

① カセットテープ kasetto-teepu　② 消しゴム keshigomu

3. Substitution drill: Asking readings

A：あの、すみません。
　　あれは何て読むんですか。

B：（禁煙）です。

A：（禁煙）？（No smoking）？

B：そう。

A: Ano, sumimasen.
　　Are wa nan te yomu'n desu ka.

B: (Kin'en) desu.

A: (Kin'en) ? '(No smoking)' ?

B: Soo.

例 Ree : 禁煙 kin'en no smoking
　　① 危険 kiken danger　② 地下鉄 chikatetsu subway　③ 駅 eki station

福 Fukubukuro

1. Socializing

How to find opportunities to make friends with Japanese people in your company/community

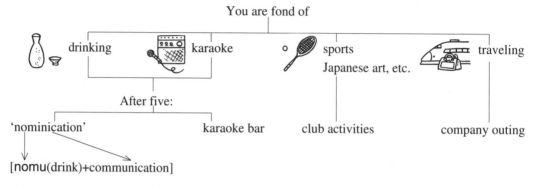

You are fond of

drinking   karaoke   sports / Japanese art, etc.   traveling

After five:

'nominication'   karaoke bar   club activities   company outing

[nomu(drink)+communication]

How to say what you are fond of:

わたしはカラオケが好きなんですが…

Watashi wa karaoke ga sukina'n desu ga…

As I like karaoke...

In a company there are bound to be people with different hobbies. Talk to the people around you at work and tell them what you like to do. This may be a new way for you to make friends at work.

2. Useful signs

The following are Chinese characters frequently found in a factory. Identify the characters, the pronunciations and the meanings that correspond to each other.

例 Ree：禁煙 ・・① はくせんないほこう hakusennai-hokoo ・・a. No smoking
(1) 立入禁止 ・・② こうおんちゅうい kooon-chuui ・・b. Off limits
(2) 高温注意 ・・③ きんえん kin'en ・・c. Caution: dangerously hot
(3) 頭上注意 ・・④ トラックでいりちゅうい torakku-deiri-chuui ・・d. Mind your head
(4) 整理整頓 ・・⑤ たちいりきんし tachiiri-kinshi ・・e. Keep tidy
(5) 白線内歩行 ・・⑥ せいりせいとん seeri-seeton ・・f. Keep within white lines
(6) トラック出入り注意 ・・⑦ ずじょうちゅうい zujoo-chuui ・・g. Watch out for vehicles

12

病気　Byooki
<small>びょう　き</small>

Falling Ill

👀 Dialogues

I. At work/Describing your problem

佐藤：李さん、どうしたんですか。
李：ええ、おなかが痛いんです。
佐藤：熱は？
李：<u>ねつ？</u>
　　str. 1-5, p. 106
佐藤：<u>ここ、熱いですか。</u>*(She touches*
　　str. 4-2, p. 107

　　Ms. Li's forehead.)
李：はい。
佐藤：ああ、熱いですね。きょうは
　　もう帰ったほうがいいですよ。
李：ええ、でも…
佐藤：顔色も悪いから、無理しない
　　ほうがいいですよ。
李：はい、すみません。
佐藤：お大事に。
李：どうも。

Satoo: Ri-san, dooshita'n desu ka.
Ri:　　Ee, onaka ga itai'n desu.
Satoo: Netsu wa?
Ri:　　<u>Netsu?</u>
　　　　str. 1-5, p. 106
Satoo: <u>Koko, atsui desu ka.</u>
　　　　str. 4-2, p. 107

　　　　(She touches Ms. Li's forehead.)
Ri:　　Hai.
Satoo: Aa, atsui desu ne. Kyoo wa moo
　　　　kaetta hoo ga ii desu yo.
Ri:　　Ee, demo…
Satoo: Kaoiro mo warui kara, muri-
　　　　shinai hoo ga ii desu yo.
Ri:　　Hai, sumimasen.
Satoo: O-daiji ni.
Ri:　　Doomo.

152

Sato: Ms. Li, what's the matter?
Li:　 I have a stomachache.
Sato: Are you feverish?
Li:　 Feverish?
Sato: Are you hot here? *(She touches Ms. Li's*
　　　 forehead.)
Li:　 Yes.
Sato: Oh, yes, you have a temperature. It's
　　　 better for you to stop working and go
　　　 home today.
Li:　 Yes, but...
Sato: You also look pale. You should really
　　　 go home.
Li:　 Yes. O.K.
Sato: Take care.
Li:　 Thank you.

おなか onaka stomach 痛い itai hurt 熱 netsu temperature/fever 熱い atsui hot 帰ります kaerimasu go
home 顔色が悪い kaoiro ga warui look pale 無理します muri-shimasu strain oneself お大事に。O-daiji ni.
Take care.

II. Finding a doctor

李 ：高橋さん、耳が痛いんですけど、お医者さん知りませんか。

高橋：耳が痛いんですか。じゃ、耳鼻科ですね。ええと、郵便局の近くに山田医院ていうお医者さんがありますよ。

李 ：そのお医者さんは中国語を話しますか。

高橋：さあ、どうかしら。

李 ：高橋さん、すみませんけど、いっしょに行ってください。

高橋：ええ、いいですよ。

Ri: Takahashi-san, mimi ga itai'n desu kedo, o-isha-san shirimasen ka.

Takahashi: Mimi ga itai'n desu ka. Ja, jibika desu ne. Eeto, yuubinkyoku no chikaku ni Yamada-iin te iu o-isha-san ga arimasu yo.

Ri: Sono o-isha-san wa Chuugoku-go o hanashimasu ka.

Takahashi: Saa, doo kashira.

Ri: Takahashi-san, sumimasen kedo, issho ni itte kudasai.

Takahashi: Ee, ii desu yo.

Li: Ms. Takahashi, I have earache. Do you know any clinics?

Takahashi: You have earache? You should go to an E.N.T. doctor, then. Well, there is a Yamada Clinic near the post office.

Li: Does the doctor speak Chinese?

Takahashi: I wonder.

Li: Ms. Takahashi, would you please come with me?

Takahashi: Sure, I will.

153

耳 mimi ear　けど kedo and　（お）医者（さん）(o-)isha(-san) doctor　耳鼻科 jibika E.N.T. doctor　郵便局 yuubinkyoku post office　近く chikaku near　～医院 ～-iin ～ clinic　中国語 Chuugoku-go Chinese　話します hanashimasu speak　どうかしら doo kashira I wonder　いっしょに issho ni (together) with

☻ Grammatical Notes

1. Parts of the body

Memorize the Japanese words for parts of the body.

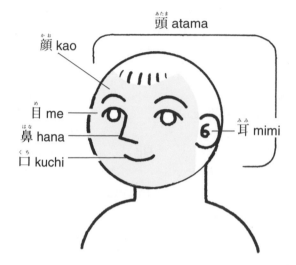

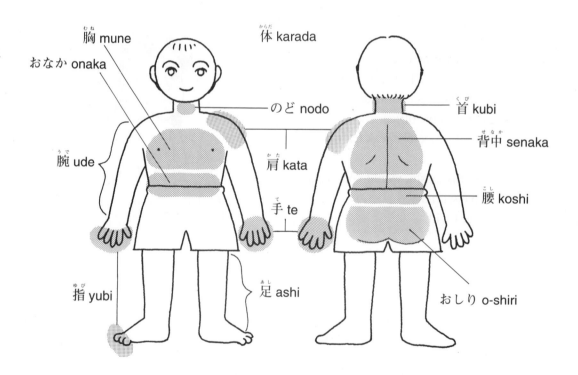

体 karada body　頭 atama head　顔 kao face　目 me eye　鼻 hana nose　口 kuchi mouth　首 kubi neck　のど nodo throat　肩 kata shoulder　背中 senaka back　胸 mune chest　腕 ude arm　手 te hand　足 ashi leg　指 yubi finger　おしり o-shiri bottom

2. Words for illness and injury

(1) （　　　　　）が痛いんです。　　（　　　　　　）ga itai'n desu.

① おなか　onaka　② 頭　atama　③ 歯　ha　④ のど　nodo

(2) 熱があります。　Netsu ga arimasu.

(3) （　　　　　）が出ます。　　（　　　　　　）ga demasu.

① せき　seki　　② はな　hana

155

(4) けがをしました。　Kega o shimashita.

① 頭を打ちました。　② 指を切りました。　③ 足を折りました。
Atama o uchimashita.　Yubi o kirimashita.　Ashi o orimashita.

(5) かゆいです。　Kayui desu.

せき seki cough　はな hana nasal mucus　けが kega injury　打ちました uchimashita hit　切りました
kirimashita cut　折りました orimashita be broken　かゆい kayui itchy

3. 〜たほうがいいです。/〜ないほうがいいです。
〜ta hoo ga ii desu./〜nai hoo ga ii desu. (Giving advice)

These expressions are used for giving advice.

Affirmative: ta-form of a verb + hoo ga ii desu = better to do
The phrase hoo ga ii desu is preceded by the ta-form of a verb. The ta-form is made by altering
the te/de of a verb in the te-form into ta/da.

masu-form	te-form	ta-form
帰ります	帰って	帰った
kaerimasu	kaette	kaetta
飲みます	飲んで	飲んだ
nomimasu	nonde	nonda

① ② ③ ④

① 病院に行きます → 行った
   Byooin ni ikimasu → itta

② 薬を飲みます → 飲んだ
   Kusuri o nomimasu → nonda

③ 休みます → 休んだ
   Yasumimasu → yasunda

④ 手術します → 手術した
   Shujutsu-shimasu → shujutsu-shita

+ ほうがいいです。
  hoo ga ii desu.

Negative: nai-form of a verb + hoo ga ii desu = better not to do
For the nai-form of verbs, see Lesson 13.

① ② ③

① お酒を飲みます → 飲まない
   O-sake o nomimasu → nomanai

② たばこを吸います → 吸わない
   Tabako o suimasu → suwanai

③ おふろに入ります → 入らない
   O-furo ni hairimasu → hairanai

+ ほうがいいです。
  hoo ga ii desu.

病院 byooin clinic/hospital 薬 kusuri medicine/drug 休みます yasumimasu take a rest 手術します shujutsu-shimasu have an operation たばこ tabako cigarette 吸います suimasu smoke （お）ふろ (o-)furo bath 入ります hairimasu enter

156

✎ Exercises

1. Substitution drill: Explaining what is wrong

(1)
A：どうしたんですか。　　A: Dooshita'n desu ka.
B：（頭）が痛いんです。　　B: (Atama) ga itai'n desu.

例 Ree : 頭 atama　① おなか onaka　② 目 me　　③ 歯 ha　　④ 耳 mimi

(2)
A：どうしたんですか。　　A: Dooshita'n desu ka.
B：（熱があるんです。）　　B: (Netsu ga aru'n desu.)

例 Ree : 熱がある　　① はなが出る　　② かゆい
　　　　　netsu ga aru　　hana ga deru　　kayui

③ 指を切った　　④ 足を折った
　 yubi o kitta　　 ashi o otta

2. Substitution drill: Giving advice

A：おなかが痛いんです。　　　　　　A: Onaka ga itai'n desu.
B：（きょうは帰った）ほうがいいですよ。　B: (Kyoo wa kaetta) hoo ga ii desu yo.

例 Ree : きょうは帰ります kyoo wa kaerimasu
(1) 病院に行きます byooin ni ikimasu
(2) ごはんを食べません gohan o tabemasen
(3) 薬を飲みます kusuri o nomimasu
(4) 今晩はお酒を飲みません konban wa o-sake o nomimasen

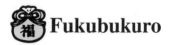 **Fukubukuro**

1. Related words

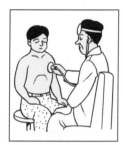

内科
naika
internal medicine
a physician

整形外科
seekee-geka
orthopedics
an orthopedist

眼科
ganka
ophthalmology
an ophthalmologist

耳鼻科
jibika
ear, nose and throat
an E.N.T. doctor

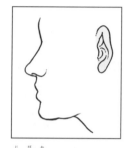

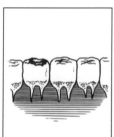

歯科
shika
dentistry
a dentist

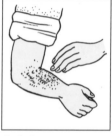

皮膚科
hifuka
dermatology
a dermatologist

2. Hospital reception

Assume that you are a receptionist at a hospital. Outpatients will tell you their problems, and you have to tell them which department they should go to.

Example:
Outpatient:　歯が痛いんです。　　　　　　Ha ga itai'n desu.
Receptionist:歯が痛いんですね。　　　　　Ha ga itai'n desu ne.
　　　　　　じゃ、歯科に行ってください。　Ja, shika ni itte kudasai.

(1) 目が痛いんです。　　　　　　　Me ga itai'n desu.
(2) 体がかゆいんです。　　　　　　Karada ga kayui'n desu.
(3) 足を折ったんです。　　　　　　Ashi o otta'n desu.
(4) せきと鼻水が出るんです。　　　Seki to hanamizu ga deru'n desu.
(5) のどが痛いんです。　　　　　　Nodo ga itai'n desu.

13

髪を切る　Kami o Kiru

かみ　き

Having a Haircut

👀 Dialogues

Ⅰ. At the hairdresser's/Asking the price

店　員：いらっしゃいませ。
リ　サ：あのう、カットはおいくらで
　　　　すか。
店　員：ええと、3,000円ですが。
リ　サ：3,000円ですか。

Ten'in: Irasshaimase.
Risa:　Anoo, katto wa o-ikura desu ka.
Ten'in: Eeto, 3,000-en desu ga.
Risa:　3,000-en desu ka.

Hairdresser:	Welcome.
Lisa:	Hello. How much do you charge for a haircut?
Hairdresser:	Well, it's 3,000 yen.
Lisa:	3,000 yen.

Ⅱ. Deciding to leave

リ　サ：どのくらい待ちますか。
店　員：そうですねえ…、ちょっと込
　　　　んでいますので、40分ぐらい
　　　　お待ちいただかないと。
リ　サ：えっ、40分ですか。じゃ、ま
　　　　　str. 2-1, p. 107
　　　　た今度。
店　員：そうですか。どうもすみませ
　　　　ん。またお願いします。
リ　サ：どうも。*(She leaves the shop.)*

Risa:　Donokurai machimasu ka.
Ten'in: Soo desu nee…, chotto konde
　　　　imasu node, 40-pun gurai o-
　　　　machi itadakanai to.
Risa:　E, 40-pun desu ka. Ja, mata
　　　　　str. 2-1, p. 107
　　　　kondo.
Ten'in: Soo desu ka. Doomo sumimasen.
　　　　Mata onegai-shimasu.
Risa:　Doomo.　*(She leaves the shop.)*

Lisa:	How long will I have to wait?
Hairdresser:	Let me see. We are rather busy now. I am afraid you will have to wait for 40 minutes.
Lisa:	What? 40 minutes? O.K. Another time, then.
Hairdresser:	I'm sorry. Please come again.
Lisa:	Thanks. *(She leaves the shop.)*

160

いらっしゃいませ。Irasshaimase. Welcome. カット katto cut （お）いくら (o-)ikura how much ええと eeto well どのくらい donokurai how long 待ちます machimasu wait そうですねえ。Soo desu nee. Let me see. ちょっと chotto a little/somewhat/rather 込んでいます konde imasu busy ので node because ぐらい gurai about お待ちいただかないと。O-machi itadakanai to. I have to ask you to wait. えっ e What! じゃ ja then また mata again 今度 kondo another time そうですか。Soo desu ka. Is that so? すみません。Sumimasen. Sorry/Excuse me. お願いします onegai-shimasu please どうも。Doomo. Thanks.

Ⅲ. Deciding to stay

リ　サ：	どのくらい待ちますか。
店　員：	そうですねえ…、10分ぐらいだと思いますが。
リ　サ：	<u>10分</u>。じゃ、お願いします。 *str. 2-1, p. 107*
店　員：	はい。お名前は？
リ　サ：	リサです。
店　員：	リサ様ですね。こちらでお待ちください。 *(She indicates a sofa.)*

Risa:　Donokurai machimasu ka.

Ten'in:　Soo desu nee, 10-pun gurai da to omoimasu ga.

Risa:　<u>10-pun</u>. Ja, onegai-shimasu.
str. 2-1, p. 107

Ten'in:　Hai. O-namae wa?

Risa:　Risa desu.

Ten'in:　Risa-sama desu ne. Kochira de o-machi kudasai. *(She indicates a sofa.)*

Lisa:	How long will I have to wait?
Hairdresser:	Well, let me see. I think you will have to wait about 10 minutes.
Lisa:	10 minutes. All right, I'll wait.
Hairdresser:	May I have your name?
Lisa:	It's Lisa.
Hairdresser:	Lisa. Would you please wait here? *(She indicates a sofa.)*

161

～と思います ～ to omoimasu think　（お）名前 (o-)namae name　～様 ～-sama Mr./Ms.～　～ですね。～ desu ne. Right?　こちら kochira this way/here　で de at　お待ちください。O-machi kudasai. Please wait.

Ⅳ. Saying what you want

店員： カットはどんな感じにしますか。

リ　サ： *(Showing a picture)* この写真のよう
　　　　にしてください。

Ten'in: Katto wa donna kanji ni shimasu ka.

Risa: *(Showing a picture)* Kono shashin no yoo ni shite kudasai.

Hairdresser:　How would you like to have your hair cut?

Lisa:　*(Showing a picture)* I would like to have my hair cut like this.

Ⅴ. Making a request

リ　サ： あ、すみません。前はあまり
　　　　str. 5-1, p. 107
　　　　切らないでください。

店員： あ、わかりました。 *(She cuts a little.)* このくらいですか。

リ　サ： ええ、そのくらいで結構です。

Risa:　A, sumimasen.
　　　　str. 5-1, p. 107
　　　　Mae wa amari kiranai de kudasai.

Ten'in: A, wakarimashita. *(She cuts a little.)* Konokurai desu ka.

Risa:　Ee, sonokurai de kekkoo desu.

162

Lisa:　Oh, please don't cut the front hair too much.

Hairdresser:　All right. *(She cuts a little.)* Will this do?

Lisa:　That's fine.

どんな donna how 感じ kanji impression します shimasu do/make この kono this 写真 shashin picture よ
うに yoo ni like あ a oh 前 mae front あまり amari (not) much 切ります kirimasu cut わかりました。
Wakarimashita. O.K. このくらい konokurai this much ええ ee yes そのくらい sonokurai that much 結構
kekkoo fine

 **Grammatical Notes**

1. 〜ないでください。 〜**nai de kudasai. (Please don't 〜.)**

This is an expression for asking someone not to do something.

切らないでください。　 Kiranai de kudasai.　　Don't cut (it), please.

使わないでください。　 Tsukawanai de kudasai.　Don't use (it), please.

The underlined verbs in the sentences above are followed by nai and are therefore called verbs in the nai-form. The sentence pattern consists of the nai-form + nai de kudasai.

The way of making the nai-form from the masu-form depends on the verb group. For the verb groups, see page 26.

The table below shows how to make the nai-form for each group.

	ます形	ない形
I	書き（ます）	書か（ない）
	急ぎ	急が
	飲み	飲ま
	呼び	呼ば
	切り	切ら
	使い	使わ
	待ち	待た
	話し	話さ
II	食べ	食べ
	寝	寝
	起き	起き
III	来	来
	し	し

	masu-form	nai-form
I	kaki(masu)	kaka(nai)
	isogi	isoga
	nomi	noma
	yobi	yoba
	kiri	kira
	tsukai	tsukawa
	machi	mata
	hanashi	hanasa
II	tabe	tabe
	ne	ne
	oki	oki
III	ki	ko
	shi	shi

163

2. ～にします。 ～ ni shimasu. (Telling your desired style)

どんな感じにしますか。
Donna kanji ni shimasu ka.
How would you like to have your hair done?

こんな感じにしてください。
Konna kanji ni shite kudasai.
I would like it made to look like this.

この写真のようにしてください。
Kono shashin no yoo ni shite kudasai.
I would like to have it done like this picture.

マイケル・ジャクソンのようにしてください。
Maikeru Jakuson no yoo ni shite kudasai.
I would like to have it made to look like Michael Jackson's.

3. このくらい konokurai (Showing how much)

This word means 'this much.' As shown in the box, there are four associated words.

これ → このくらい	kore → konokurai	this much
それ → そのくらい	sore → sonokurai	that much
あれ → あのくらい	are → anokurai	that much
どれ → どのくらい	dore → donokurai	how much

どのくらい切りますか。
Donokurai kirimasu ka.
How much shall I cut?

このくらいお願いします。
Konokurai onegai-shimasu.
Would you cut this much?

このくらいですか。
Konokurai desu ka.
This much?

ええ、そのくらいです。
Ee, sonokurai desu.
Yes, that much.

マイケル・ジャクソン Maikeru Jakuson Michael Jackson

✏️ Exercises

1. Substitution drill: Asking the price

店　員：いらっしゃいませ。	Ten'in: Irasshaimase.
あなた：（カット）は、おいくらですか。	Anata: (Katto) wa, o-ikura desu ka.
店　員：（カット）ですか。	Ten'in: (Katto) desu ka.
（2,500円）ですが。	(2,500-en) desu ga.
あなた：（2,500円）。	Anata: (2,500-en).
じゃ、お願いします。	Ja, onegai-shimasu.

例 Ree：カット　katto,　2,500円 2,500-en
　① パーマ　paama,　5,000円 5,000-en　② セット　setto,　3,000円 3,000-en

2. Substitution drill: Asking how long

あなた：どのくらい待ちますか。	Anata: Donokurai machimasu ka.
店　員：そうですねえ。	Ten'in: Soo desu nee.
（30分）ぐらいだと思いますが。	(30-pun) gurai da to omoimasu ga.

(able to wait)	(not able to wait)
あなた：（30分）。じゃ、お願いします。	あなた：（30分）。じゃ、また今度。
店　員：はい。こちらでお待ちください。	店　員：そうですか。どうもすみません。
Anata: (30-pun). Ja, onegai-shimasu.	またお願いします。
Ten'in: Hai. Kochira de o-machi kudasai.	Anata: (30-pun). Ja, mata kondo.
	Ten'in: Soo desu ka. Doomo sumimasen.
	Mata onegai-shimasu.

165

例 Ree：30分 30-pun　① 10分 10-pun　② 1時間 1-jikan

3. Substitution drill: Making requests

あなた：あ、すみません。（前）はあまり	Anata: A, sumimasen. (Mae) wa amari
切らないでください。	kiranai de kudasai.
店　員：あ、わかりました。	Ten'in: A, wakarimashita.
このくらいですか。	Konokurai desu ka.
あなた：ええ、そのくらいで結構です。	Anata: Ee, sonokurai de kekkoo desu.

例 Ree：前 mae 　① 横 yoko 　② 後ろ ushiro

パーマ paama perm　セット setto set　横 yoko side　後ろ ushiro back

4. Match each picture with the right request.

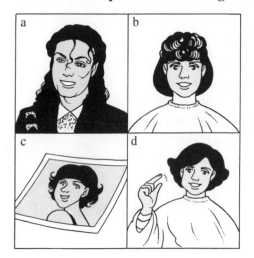

(1) この写真のようにしてください。
Kono shashin no yoo ni shite kudasai. (　　)

(2) マイケル・ジャクソンのようにしてください。
Maikeru Jakuson no yoo ni shite kudasai. (　　)

(3) このくらい切ってください。
Konokurai kitte kudasai. (　　)

(4) 前だけパーマをかけてください。
Mae dake paama o kakete kudasai. (　　)

5. Match each picture with the right request.

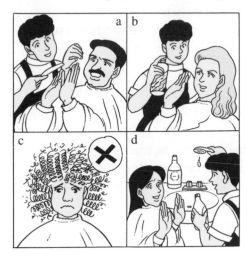

(1) スプレーは使わないでください。
Supuree wa tsukawanai de kudasai. (　　)

(2) シャンプーはしないでください。
Shanpuu wa shinai de kudasai. (　　)

(3) ひげはそらないでください。
Hige wa soranai de kudasai. (　　)

(4) パーマは強くかけないでください。
Paama wa tsuyoku kakenai de kudasai. (　　)

166

だけ dake only　かけます kakemasu have a perm　スプレー supuree spray　シャンプー shanpuu shampoo
ひげ hige beard, mustache　そります sorimasu shave　強く tsuyoku strongly

福 Fukubukuro

1. Useful words

例 Ree : シャンプー ・   ・① katto ・   ・ a. set

(1) カット ・   ・② paama ・   ・ b. perm

(2) セット ・   ・③ buroo ・   ・ c. shampoo

(3) パーマ ・   ・④ setto ・   ・ d. cut

(4) ブロー ・   ・⑤ shanpuu ・   ・ e. blow-dry

(5) ヘアダイ ・   ・⑥ headai ・   ・ f. hair dye

2. Useful expressions

Here are some expressions used at the hairdresser's.

Reception:

あなた：シャンプーは料金に入っていますか。   Anata: Shanpuu wa ryookin ni haitte imasu ka.

店 員：いいえ、シャンプーは別料金です。   Ten'in: Iie, shanpuu wa betsu-ryookin desu.

あなた：じゃ、シャンプーは結構です。   Anata: Ja, shanpuu wa kekkoo desu.

店 員：お荷物、お預かりします。   Ten'in: O-nimotsu, o-azukari shimasu.

You:　　　Does the price include a shampoo?

Hairdresser: No, the cost of a shampoo is not
　　　　　　included.

You:　　　Then a shampoo is not necessary.

Hairdresser: We'll keep your things.

167

Shampoo:

店 員：熱くないですか。   Ten'in: Atsukunai desu ka.

あなた：はい、ちょうどいいです。   Anata: Hai, choodo ii desu.

あなた：ちょっと熱いです。   Anata: Chotto atsui desu.

Hairdresser: Isn't it hot?

You:　　　No, it's fine.

You:　　　Yes, it's rather hot.

Cut:

店 員：分け目はどこですか。   Ten'in: Wakeme wa doko desu ka.

あなた：ここにしてください。   Anata: Koko ni shite kudasai.

Hairdresser: Where would you like to have a
　　　　　　parting?

You:　　　Here, please.

Blow-dry:

店　員：前髪は下ろしますか。

あなた：上げてください。

Ten'in: Maegami wa oroshimasu ka.

Anata: Agete kudasai.

Hairdresser: Would you like to wear your front hair up, or would you prefer it down?

You: Make it up, please.

Finishing:

店　員：いかがですか。

あなた：はい、結構です。どうも。

店　員：お疲れさまでした。

Ten'in: Ikaga desu ka.

Anata: Hai, kekkoo desu. Doomo.

Ten'in: Otsukaresama deshita.

Hairdresser: How is it?

You: It's fine. Thank you.

Hairdresser: Thank you.

14

訪問する　Hoomon-suru

ほうもん

Visiting People

🫁 Dialogues

Ⅰ. At the front door/Visiting your superior

李 ： *(She rings the door bell.)*
　　ごめんください。李です。

佐 藤：はい。 *(The door opens.)* ああ、い
　　らっしゃい。どうぞ。

李 ：こんにちは。お邪魔します。
　　(She enters.)

Ri: *(She rings the door bell.)* Gomenkudasai. Ri desu.

Satoo: Hai. *(The door opens.)* Aa, irasshai.
Doozo.

Ri: Konnichiwa. O-jama-shimasu.
(She enters.)

Li: *(She rings the door bell.)* Hello. It's Li.
Sato: Yes. *(The door opens.)* Oh, welcome, Ms. Li. Please come in.
Li: Good afternoon, Ms. Sato. Excuse me.
(She enters.)

Ⅱ. In the entrance way/Asking dos and don'ts

李 ： *(Noting shoes at the entrance)* あのう、
　　靴は…

佐 藤：あ、靴はここで脱いでくださ
　　いね。

李 ：ここですか。
　　str. 2-1, p. 107

佐 藤：ええ。このスリッパ、使って。

李 ：はい、すみません。

Ri: *(Noting shoes at the entrance)* Anoo,
kutsu wa…

Satoo: A, kutsu wa koko de nuide
kudasai ne.

Ri: Koko desu ka.
str. 2-1, p. 107

Sato: Ee. Kono surippa, tsukatte.

Ri: Hai, sumimasen.

Li: *(Noting shoes at the entrance)* Should I take off...
Sato: Yes, please take off your shoes here.
Li: Here?
Sato: Yes. And would you put on these slippers?
Li: Thank you.

ごめんください。 Gomenkudasai. Hello. <greeting used at the entrance of someone's house> いらっしゃい。
Irasshai. Welcome. どうぞ。 Doozo. Please (come in). お邪魔します。 O-jama-shimasu. Excuse me.
<expression used when entering someone's house> 靴 kutsu shoes 脱ぎます nugimasu take off ここ koko
here スリッパ surippa slippers 使って tsukatte <informal way of saying 'Please use.'>

Ⅲ. In the living room/Paying compliments

李 ：*(Looking around the room)* きれいで
　　　すね。
佐藤：いいえ、もう古いんですよ。
　　　どうぞ、かけてください。
李 ：あ、どうも。

Ri: 　　*(Looking around the room)* Kiree desu
　　　ne.
Satoo: Iie, moo furui'n desu yo. Doozo,
　　　kakete kudasai.
Ri: 　　A, doomo.

Li: 　*(Looking around the room)* It's a nice
　　　house.
Sato: Oh, it's an old place. Please sit down.
Li: 　Oh, thank you.

Ⅳ. Handing over a gift

李 ：あのう、これ、中国のお菓子
　　　です。どうぞ。
佐藤：え、すみませんねえ。いいん
　　　ですか。
李 ：ええ、どうぞ。
佐藤：じゃ、遠慮なく、頂きますね。
　　　どうもありがとう。
李 ：いいえ。

Ri: 　　Anoo, kore, Chuugoku no o-
　　　kashi desu. Doozo.
Satoo: E, sumimasen nee. Ii'n desu ka.
Ri: 　　Ee, doozo.
Satoo: Ja, enryo-naku itadakimasu ne.
　　　Doomo arigatoo.
Ri: 　　Iie.

171

Li: 　I've brought you a Chinese cake.
Sato: Oh, really?
Li: 　Yes. Please take it.
Sato: That's very nice of you. Thank you.
Li: 　My pleasure.

きれい［な］ kiree[na] beautiful/nice もう moo already 古い furui old かけます kakemasu sit お菓子 o-kashi cake 遠慮なく enryo-naku without being reserved 頂きます itadakimasu accept <humble form of moraimasu>

Ⅴ. Eating

佐藤：和菓子、食べたこと、ある？
　李　：いいえ、ありません。
佐藤：じゃ、どうぞ、食べてみて。
　李　：いただきます。*(She eats.)* とても
　　　　甘いですね。

Satoo: Wagashi, tabeta koto, aru?
Ri:　　Iie, arimasen.
Satoo: Ja, doozo, tabete mite.
Ri:　　Itadakimasu. *(She eats.)* Totemo
　　　　amai desu ne.

Sato: Have you tried Japanese cakes before?
Li:　　No, I haven't.
Sato: Why don't you try some?
Li:　　Thank you. *(She eats.)* It's very sweet.

Ⅵ. Saying goodbye

　李　：*(Looking at her watch)* あ、もう5時。
　　　　そろそろ失礼します。
佐藤：えっ、もっとゆっくりしてい
　　　　ったら。
　李　：ええ、ありがとうございます。
　　　　でももう遅いので。
佐藤：そう。残念ですね。
　李　：きょうはどうもごちそうさま
　　　　でした。
佐藤：いいえ。じゃ、気をつけて。

Ri:　　*(Looking at her watch)* A, moo 5-ji.
　　　　Sorosoro shitsuree-shimasu.
Satoo: E, motto yukkuri-shite ittara.
Ri:　　Ee, arigatoo gozaimasu. Demo
　　　　moo osoi node.
Satoo: Soo. Zannen desu ne.
Ri:　　Kyoo wa doomo gochisoosama
　　　　deshita.
Satoo: Iie. Ja, ki o tsukete.

Li:　　*(Looking at her watch)* Oh, it's already
　　　　five o'clock. I must be going now.
Sato: Oh, it's too early. Please stay more.
Li:　　Thank you, but it's almost time that I
　　　　left.
Sato: That's a pity.
Li:　　Thank you for your hospitality today.
Sato: You are welcome. Please take care.

和菓子 wagashi Japanese cake 食べます tabemasu eat いただきます。Itadakimasu. <set phrase used before eating or drinking> とても totemo very 甘い amai sweet そろそろ失礼します。Sorosoro shitsuree-shimasu. It's almost time to leave. <expression used to say that you are going to leave> もっと motto more ゆっくりします yukkuri-shimasu take time でも demo but 遅い osoi late 残念 zannen pity きょう kyoo today ごちそうさま。Gochisoosama. Thank you for the delicious meal/cake. <set phrase used after eating and drinking> 気をつけて。Ki o tsukete. Take care.

Grammatical Notes

1. 〜たことがあります。 〜**ta koto ga arimasu.** (**Expressing experience**)

When talking about experience, a sentence consisting of the ta-form of a verb + koto ga arimasu is used. The ta-form is made from the te-form. (Examples: mite → mita, itte → itta. See Lesson 12.)

> 食べたことがありますか。
> Tabeta koto ga arimasu ka.
> Have you eaten this before?
> （食べたことある？
> Tabeta koto aru?)

> ええ、あります。
> 大好きです。
> Ee, arimasu.
> Daisuki desu.
> Yes, I have.
> I like it very much.

> いいえ、ありません。これは何ですか。
> Iie, arimasen.
> Kore wa nan desu ka.
> No, I haven't.
> What is it?

> ええ、あります。でもちょっと…
> Ee, arimasu. Demo chotto…
> Yes, I have, but actually I...

173

飲みます	→	飲んだことがあります。
nomimasu	→	Nonda koto ga arimasu.
drink	→	I've drunk that.
見ます	→	見たことがあります。
mimasu	→	Mita koto ga arimasu.
see	→	I've seen that.
行きます	→	行ったことがあります。
ikimasu	→	Itta koto ga arimasu.
go	→	I've been there.

飲みます nomimasu drink 見ます mimasu see 行きます ikimasu go

2. 〜てみます。 〜te mimasu. (try 〜ing)

A sentence consisting of the te-form of a verb + mimasu means 'try 〜ing.' For the te-form, see Lesson 10.

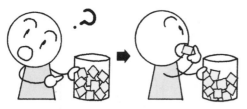

これは何ですか。　　食べてみます。
Kore wa nan desu ka.　Tabete mimasu.
What are these?　　　I'll try one.

これはどんな本ですか。　　読んでみます。
Kore wa donna hon desu ka.　Yonde mimasu.
What sort of book is this?　　I'll try reading it.

これは何ですか。　　飲んでみます。
Kore wa nan desu ka.　Nonde mimasu.
What is this?　　　　I'll try it.

Use the following to recommend food.

食べてみてください。	Tabete mite kudasai.	Please try. (Formal)
食べてみて。	Tabete mite.	Try. (Informal)

本 hon book

Exercises

1. Substitution drill: Talking about food

佐　藤：（和菓子）、食べたこと、ある？	Satoo:　(Wagashi), tabeta koto, aru?
あなた：⌈ええ、あります。	Anata:⌈Ee, arimasu.
⌈ええ、あります。でも、ちょっと…	⌈Ee, arimasu. Demo, chotto…
⌊いいえ、食べたことがありません。	⌊Iie, tabeta koto ga arimasen.
（和菓子）って何ですか。	(Wagashi) tte nan desu ka.

例 Ree：和菓子 wagashi　① すき焼き sukiyaki　② すし sushi　③ 納豆 nattoo

2. Select the right words from the box for inserting in (①　) and (②　).

(1)

佐　藤：日本のお酒、（①　　　）	Satoo:　Nihon no o-sake, (①　　　)
ことがありますか。	koto ga arimasu ka.
あなた：ええ、あります。	Anata:　Ee, arimasu.
（②　　　）ですね。	(②　　　) desu ne.

(2)

佐　藤：このビデオ、（①　　　）	Satoo:　Kono bideo, (①　　　)
ことがありますか。	koto ga arimasu ka.
あなた：ええ、あります。	Anata:　Ee, arimasu.
（②　　　）ですね。	(②　　　) desu ne.

(3)

佐　藤：スキー、（①　　　）	Satoo:　Sukii, (①　　　) koto
ことがありますか。	ga arimasu ka.
あなた：ええ、あります。	Anata:　Ee, arimasu.
（②　　　）ですね。	(②　　　) desu ne.

---

① 見た mita，飲んだ nonda，した shita
② 楽しい tanoshii，おもしろい omoshiroi，おいしい oishii

すき焼き sukiyaki sukiyaki　すし sushi sushi　納豆 nattoo natto　（お）酒 (o-)sake sake　ビデオ bideo video
スキー sukii skiing　します shimasu do　楽しい tanoshii delightful/pleasant　おもしろい omoshiroi
interesting　おいしい oishii delicious

3. Conjugate the verbs and use them to complete the dialogue.

田中：これ、（食べた）こと、ある？　　　Tanaka: Kore, (tabeta) koto aru?
　李　：いいえ、ありません。　　　　　　Ri:　　 Iie, arimasen.
田中：じゃ、どうぞ、（食べて）みて。　　Tanaka: Ja, doozo, (tabete) mite.

例 Ree：食べます tabemasu
　　　(1) 読みます yomimasu　　(2) 飲みます nomimasu　　(3) 聞きます kikimasu

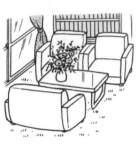  

4. Match each picture with the right compliment.

例 Ree：（①　　）　　　(1) (　　　)　　　(2) (　　　)　　　(3) (　　　)

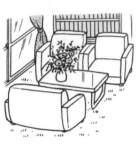

① きれいですね。	Kiree desu ne.
② かわいいですね。	Kawaii desu ne.
③ おいしいですね。	Oishii desu ne.
④ すごいですね。	Sugoi desu ne.

176

かわいい kawaii cute　すごい sugoi amazing

 **Fukubukuro**

1. Adjectives of taste

甘い	amai	sweet
辛い	karai	hot
塩辛い	shiokarai	salty
苦い	nigai	bitter
酸っぱい	suppai	sour
おいしい	oishii	delicious/tasty

2. What would you do if...

(1) Suppose that you as a guest said you would be leaving now and your host/hostess asked you to stay longer. What would you say to him/her?

でもちょっと寄るところがあるので。
Demo chotto yoru tokoro ga aru node.
Thank you, but I have to visit someone.

でも子どもが待っているので。
Demo kodomo ga matte iru node.
Thank you, but my children are now waiting for me.

じゃ、もう少しだけ。
Ja, moo sukoshi dake.
O.K., just for a little while, then.

もっとゆっくりしていったら。
Motto yukkuri-shite ittara.
I wish you'd stay longer.

(2) The customs and manners to be observed when visiting someone differ from country to country. Compare the following customs with those of your own country. Ask for comments from your Japanese/non-Japanese friends and colleagues.

Yes (Y)　　　　No (N)　　　Don't know (-)

· When you intend visiting someone, you should tell them beforehand. (　　)
· You may visit someone as early as 8 o'clock in the morning. (　　)
· You are supposed to eat all that is served. (　　)
· You are supposed to help your host/hostess with cooking or clearing the table. (　　)
· When you are asked to stay longer, you should accept. (　　)
· When your guest has brought you a gift, you should decline it at first. (　　)
· A gift that you have received should be opened on the spot. (　　)
· When the gift you have received is food, you should open it immediately and share it with the giver. (　　)

15

<ruby>宗教<rt>しゅうきょう</rt></ruby> Shuukyoo

Religion

👀 Dialogues

Ⅰ. At work/Explaining religious customs

鈴　木：じゃ、お疲れさん、またあした。

ア　リ：<u>すみません</u>、あしたはお祈り
str. 5-1, p. 107
　　　　に行きたいんですが。

鈴　木：えっ、あした来られないの？

ア　リ：ええ、あしたはとても大切な日
　　　　なんです。

鈴　木：どうして？

ア　リ：あしたはイスラム教の大切な
　　　　お祭りなので、お祈りに行か
　　　　なければいけません。

鈴　木：そう、それは知らなかったな
　　　　あ。

ア　リ：お願いします。

鈴　木：わかった。今度から休む予定
　　　　はもっと早く言ってよ。

Suzuki: Ja, otsukaresan, mata ashita.

Ari: <u>Sumimasen</u>, ashita wa o-inori ni
str. 5-1, p. 107
ikitai'n desu ga.

Suzuki: E, ashita korarenai no?

Ari: Ee, ashita wa totemo taisetsuna
hi na'n desu.

Suzuki: Dooshite?

Ari: Ashita wa Isuramu-kyoo no
taisetsuna o-matsuri na node, o-
inori ni ikanakereba ikemasen.

Suzuki: Soo, sore wa shiranakatta naa.

Ari: Onegai-shimasu.

Suzuki: Wakatta. Kondo kara yasumu
yotee wa motto hayaku itte yo.

180

Suzuki: See you tomorrow.

Ali: Could you spare me tomorrow? I
would like to go to mosque.

Suzuki: What? Do you mean you are not
coming tomorrow?

Ali: Yes. Tomorrow is a very important
day for me.

Suzuki: Why?

Ali: Tomorrow we are going to
celebrate a very important Islamic
festival. So I have to go to mosque.

Suzuki: Oh, I didn't know that.

Ali: Please.

Suzuki: All right. But next time you should
notify me in advance when you are
going to have a day off.

お疲れさん。Otsukaresan.<Lit. I appreciate your work today.> またあした。Mata ashita. See you
tomorrow. お祈り o-inori prayer 大切［な］taisetsu[na] important イスラム教 Isuramu-kyoo Islam（お）
祭り (o-)matsuri festival 今度から kondo kara from next time 休みます yasumimasu take a day off 予定
yotee plan もっと motto more

II. At a party/Explaining about religion

田中：アリさん、1杯どうですか。
  (He tries to pour sake.)
アリ：すみません、わたし、お酒は
  だめなんです。
田中：だめ？どこか悪いんですか。
アリ：いいえ。
田中：じゃ、1杯だけ、いいでしょ。
アリ：すみません、お酒は飲めない
  んです。
田中：どうして？
アリ：わたしはイスラム教徒なので、
  お酒を飲んではいけないんです。
田中：そうですか。じゃ、ジュースは？
アリ：はい、頂きます。

Tanaka: Ari-san, 1-pai doo desu ka.
  (He tries to pour sake.)
Ari:　　Sumimasen, watashi, o-sake
  wa damena'n desu.
Tanaka: Dame? Dokoka warui'n desu ka.
Ari:　　Iie.
Tanaka: Ja, 1-pai dake, ii desho.
Ari:　　Sumimasen, o-sake wa
  nomenai'n desu.
Tanaka: Dooshite?
Ari:　　Watashi wa Isuramu-kyooto na
  node, o-sake o nonde wa
  ikenai'n desu.
Tanaka: Soo desu ka. Ja, juusu wa?
Ari:　　Hai, itadakimasu.

Tanaka: Ali, why don't you have a drink?
  (He tries to pour sake.)
Ali:　　Sorry, I don't drink alcohol.
Tanaka: Don't drink? Is there anything
  wrong with you?
Ali:　　No.
Tanaka: Then just a cup of sake won't do any
  harm.
Ali:　　Sorry, I can't drink.
Tanaka: Why?
Ali:　　Since I'm a Muslim, drinking is not
  allowed.
Tanaka: Is that so? Is juice O.K., then?
Ali:　　Yes, I'll have that.

181

1杯どうですか。 **1-pai doo desu ka.** Why don't you have a drink? どこか悪い **dokoka warui** Something is wrong with... 飲めません **nomemasen** cannot drink イスラム教徒 **Isuramu-kyooto** Muslim ジュース **juusu** juice

 **Grammatical Notes**

1. **〜ので 〜 node** (Because 〜, 〜.)

   When explaining something, you can use this expression as follows:

   > あしたお祈りに ~~行きます。~~ 行くので、休みます。
   >
   > Ashita o-inori ni ~~ikimasu.~~ iku node, yasumimasu.
   >
   > I'll take a day off tomorrow to go to mosque/church/temple.

   > 気分が悪い ~~です。~~ ので、あまり食べられません。
   >
   > Kibun ga warui ~~desu.~~ node, amari taberaremasen.
   >
   > I feel ill, so I can't eat very much.

   > あしたのお祭りは大切 ~~です。~~ なので、お祈りに行かなければいけません。
   >
   > Ashita no o-matsuri wa taisetsu ~~desu.~~ na node, o-inori ni ikanakereba ikemasen.
   >
   > Since tomorrow's festival is very important, I have to go to mosque/church/temple.

   > あしたは日曜日 ~~です。~~ なので、教会へ行きます。
   >
   > Ashita wa nichi-yoobi ~~desu.~~ na node, kyookai e ikimasu.
   >
   > As it's Sunday tomorrow, I'm going to church.

   In Lesson 7, you learned the expression Kore wa kaisoku desu kara, tomarimasen yo, which means, 'This train doesn't stop (there) because it is a rapid service train.' Both kara and node are used to give reasons, but node sounds somehow more polite than kara, particularly when you are explaining your personal situation or seeking someone's permission/consent. Note that desu after a na-adjective or a noun is changed to na when followed by node. It is possible to say desu node, but na node is used more often.

2. **〜なければいけません。 〜nakereba ikemasen.** (Expressing obligation)

   Example: お祈りに行かなければいけません。

   > O-inori ni ikanakereba ikemasen.
   >
   > I must go to mosque.

   Ikanakereba is a conjugated form of the verb ikimasu. This form is created by attaching nakereba to the nai-form of the verb (ika). There is another expression, ikanakereba narimasen, the meaning of which is the same as ikanakereba ikemasen. In colloquial Japanese, ikanakya or ikanakucha is used instead.

気分が悪い kibun ga warui feel ill　教会 kyookai church

3. ～てはいけません。 ～te wa ikemasen. (Expressing prohibition/restriction)

Example: お酒を飲んではいけません。

O-sake o nonde wa ikemasen.

You mustn't drink alcohol.

Nonde wa is a conjugated form of the verb nomimasu. This form is made by attaching wa to the end of the te-form of a verb. In colloquial Japanese, nonja can be used in place of nonde wa.

4. Potential form of verbs

When you would like to say that some action is possible, the potential form of a verb should be used.

How to make the potential form

		可 能 形					potential form	
		丁 寧 体	普 通 体				polite form	plain form
I	書き（ます）	書けます	書ける	I	kaki(masu)	kakemasu	kakeru
	急ぎ	急げます	急げる		isogi	isogemasu	isogeru
	飲み	飲めます	飲める		nomi	nomemasu	nomeru
	呼び	呼べます	呼べる		yobi	yobemasu	yoberu
	切り	切れます	切れる		kiri	kiremasu	kireru
	使い	使えます	使える		tsukai	tsukaemasu	tsukaeru
	待ち	待てます	待てる		machi	matemasu	materu
	話し	話せます	話せる		hanashi	hanasemasu	hanaseru
II	食べ	食べられます	食べられる	II	tabe	taberaremasu	taberareru
	寝	寝られます	寝られる		ne	neraremasu	nerareru
	起き	起きられます	起きられる		oki	okiraremasu	okirareru
III	来	来られます	来られる	III	ki	koraremasu	korareru
	し	できます	できる		shi	dekimasu	dekiru

Group I verbs: 飲みます → 飲めます   nomimasu → nomemasu

Change nomi to nome. Its negative form is nomemasen.

Group II verbs: 食べます → 食べられます   tabemasu → taberaremasu

After tabe, rare should be added. Its negative form is taberaremasen.

Group III verbs: します → できます   shimasu → dekimasu

来ます → 来られます   kimasu → koraremasu

The negative form of dekimasu is dekimasen. The negative form of koraremasu is koraremasen.

In colloquial Japanese, you may use an informal style, such as Ashita korarenai no? (Can't you come tomorrow?) instead of Ashita korarenai'n desu ka.

183

✍ Exercises

1. Substitution drill: Giving reasons

A：お酒は飲めないんです。   A: O-sake wa nomenai'n desu.

B：どうしてですか。   B: Dooshite desu ka.

A：わたしは（イスラム教徒なので）、   A: Watashi wa (Isuramu-kyooto na node),
   お酒は飲めないんです。   o-sake wa nomenai'n desu.

例 Ree：イスラム教徒です　Isuramu-kyooto desu
① 今、病気です　ima, byooki desu
② きょうは車です　kyoo wa kuruma desu

2. Answer the questions with your own devised reasons.

(1)

A：豚肉は食べられないんです。   A: Butaniku wa taberarenai'n desu.

B：どうしてですか。   B: Dooshite desu ka.

A：（　　　　　　　　　）   A: (　　　　　　　　　)

(2)

A：あした、お祈りに   A: Ashita, o-inori ni ikanakereba ikenai'n
   行かなければいけないんです。   desu.

B：どうしてですか。   B: Dooshite desu ka.

A：（　　　　　　　　　）   A: (　　　　　　　　　)

(3)

A：昼はごはんを食べられないんです。   A: Hiru wa gohan o taberarenai'n desu.

B：どうしてですか。   B: Dooshite desu ka.

A：（　　　　　　　　　）   A: (　　　　　　　　　)

3. Make sentences with 'nai-form + nakereba ikemasen.'

例 Ree：お祈りに行きます　o-inori ni ikimasu
    →お祈りに行かなければいけません　o-inori ni ikanakereba ikemasen

(1) 5時に起きます　5-ji ni okimasu →
(2) 薬を飲みます　kusuri o nomimasu →
(3) 帰ります　kaerimasu →

4. **Make sentences with 'te-form + wa ikemasen.'**

例 Ree：お酒を飲みます o-sake o nomimasu
→ お酒を飲んではいけません o-sake o nonde wa ikemasen

(1) 牛肉を食べます gyuuniku o tabemasu →
(2) たばこを吸います tabako o suimasu →
(3) ごみを捨てます gomi o sutemasu →

5. **Talk about your religion using 'nai-form + nakereba ikemasen' and 'te-form + wa ikemasen.'**

例：ラマダンの間、昼はごはんを食べてはいけません。
Ree：Ramadan no aida, hiru wa gohan o tabete wa ikemasen.

6. **Change the following verbs into their potential forms.**

potential form
(affirmative) → (negative)
例：来ます (group Ⅲ)   → 来られます → 来られません
Ree：kimasu (group Ⅲ) → koraremasu → koraremasen

(1) 飲みます nomimasu (group Ⅰ)
(2) 食べます tabemasu (group Ⅱ)
(3) します shimasu (group Ⅲ)

185

ごみ gomi trash 捨てます sutemasu throw away ラマダン Ramadan Ramadan

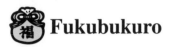 **Fukubukuro**

1. Names of different religions

宗教	shuukyoo	religion
イスラム教	Isuramu-kyoo	Islam
キリスト教	Kirisuto-kyoo	Christianity
仏教	Bukkyoo	Buddhism
ユダヤ教	Yudaya-kyoo	Judaism
モルモン教	Morumon-kyoo	Mormonism
ヒンズー教	Hinzuu-kyoo	Hinduism

Each religion has its own precepts. Look at the pictures and talk about the precepts of various religions.

2. What would you do if...

Example: Suppose that you are a Muslim and now observing Ramadan, and your friend asks you to keep him company for lunch.

いまラマダンなので、ちょっと…
Ima Ramadan na node, chotto…
I am afraid I can't; I'm observing Ramadan now.

わたしはイスラム教徒なのでいま断食をしています。
Watashi wa Isuramu-kyooto na node ima danjiki o shite imasu.
Since I am a Muslim, I am observing Ramadan now.

昼はごはんを食べてはいけません。
Hiru wa gohan o tabete wa ikemasen.
I mustn't eat during daylight hours.

Now make excuses for the following situations.

(1) You are not a Christian, but your friend is now asking you to go to church with him on Christmas Day.

(2) Your Japanese friend is asking you to go to a shrine with him on New Year's Day.

(3) Your Japanese friend is asking you to take him to mosque.

(4) You make it a rule to go to church on Sundays, but your Japanese friend is asking you to go on a tour with him on the weekend.

Answers

Lesson 1
Fukubukuro
1. (1) d (2) c (3) a (4) e (5) b

Lesson 2
Exercises
1. (1) d (2) c (3) a (4) b (5) e
2. (1) ①そこ soko ②ここ koko ③入り口の近く iriguchi no chikaku

Fukubukuro
1.1 (1) b (2) f (3) c (4) e (5) a (6) d
1.2 引

Lesson 3
Exercises
1.(1)それ、卵 sore, tamago (2)あれ、ハンバーガー are, hanbaagaa
3.(1)グラタン1つと、ピラフ1つと、ミックスサンド1つ Guratan hitotsu to, pirafu hitotsu to, mikkusu-sando hitotsu (2)ピラフ4つ Pirafu yottsu

Fukubukuro
1.1 (1) ⑥ c (2) ① e (3) ② d (4) ③ f (5) ④ b
1.2 (1) ② (2) ① (3) ③

Lesson 5
Exercises
1.(1)速達 sokutatsu (2)船便 funabin (3)書留 kakitome
2.(1)50円切手、8、400 50-en kitte, 8, 400 (2)270円切手、5、1,350 270-en kitte, 5, 1,350 (3)航空書簡、3、270 kookuu-shokan, 3, 270
3.(1)Example:
　　あなた：これ、ブラジルまで航空便でいくらですか。
　　局　員：3,200円です。
　　あなた：じゃ、船便だといくらですか。
　　局　員：2,200円です。
　　あなた：これ、ブラジルまで船便でどのくらいかかりますか。
　　局　員：1か月ぐらいです。
　　あなた：そうですか。航空便だとどのくらいかかりますか。
　　局　員：1週間ぐらいです。
　　あなた：じゃ、船便でお願いします。

Anata: Kore, Burajiru made kookuubin de ikura desu ka.

Kyokuin: 3,200-en desu.

Anata: Ja, funabin da to ikura desu ka.

Kyokuin: 2,200-en desu.

Anata: Kore, Burajiru made funabin de donokurai kakarimasu ka.

Kyokuin: 1-kagetsu gurai desu.

Anata: Soo desu ka. Kookuubin da to donokurai kakarimasu ka.

Kyokuin: 1-shuukan gurai desu.

Anata: Ja, funabin de onegai-shimasu.

Fukubukuro

1.(1) A (2) A (3) B

2.(1) b (2) b (3) a (4) b (5) b

Lesson 6

Fukubukuro

1.(1) ④ (2) ① (3) ②

3.(1) ⑤ (2) ② (3) ① (4) ④

Lesson 7

Exercises

1.(1)止まります tomarimasu (2)行きます ikimasu (3)乗ります norimasu

2.(1)止まりますか, 止まります, 止まりません   Tomarimasu ka, tomarimasu, tomarimasen

　(2)乗りますか, 乗ります, 乗りません, Norimasu ka, norimasu, norimasen

4.(1) 8つ Yattsu (2) 5つ Itsutsu (3) 6つ Muttsu

5.(1)はい、各駅停車ですから、止まりますよ。Hai, kakueki-teesha desu kara, tomarimasu yo.

　(2)いいえ、快速ですから、止まりませんよ。Iie, kaisoku desu kara, tomarimasen yo.

　(3)いいえ、快速ですから、止まりませんよ。Iie, kaisoku desu kara, tomarimasen yo.

Fukubukuro

1.(1) ① (2) ③ (3) ②

3.(1) ② e (2) ① f (3) ⑤ a (4) ③ c (5) ④ d

Lesson 8

Fukubukuro

2.(1) p.135 (2) p.153 (3) p.94 (p.116, p.118)

Lesson 9

Exercises

1.(1)アレルギーがある arerugii ga aru (2)焼き鳥を注文する yakitori o chuumon-suru
(3)野菜を食べる yasai o taberu

Fukubukuro

2.(1) ⑥ h (2) ④ a (3) ⑨ b (4) ⑦ f (5) ① c (6) ③ e (7) ⑤ j (8) ② d (9) ⑧ k (10) ⑪ i

Polite and Plain Styles

Polite 1, 2, 4 Plain 3, 5

Lesson 10

Exercises

1.(1) (b) (2) (d) (3) (a) (4) (c)

Fukubukuro

2.(1) ④ (2) ④ (3) ①

Lesson 11

Fukubukuro

2.(1) ⑤ b (2) ② c (3) ⑦ d (4) ⑥ e (5) ① f (6) ④ g

Lesson 12

Exercises

2.(1)病院に行った Byooin ni itta (2)ごはんを食べない Gohan o tabenai
(3)薬を飲んだ Kusuri o nonda (4)今晩はお酒を飲まない Konban wa o-sake o nomanai

Fukubukuro

2.(1)眼科 ganka (2)皮膚科 hifuka (3)整形外科 seekee-geka (4)内科 naika
(5)内科（耳鼻科） naika (jibika)

Lesson 13

Exercises

4.(1) c (2) a (3) d (4) b
5.(1) b (2) d (3) a (4) c

Fukubukuro

1.(1) ① d (2) ④ a (3) ② b (4) ③ e (5) ⑥ f

Lesson 14

Exercises

2.(1) ① 飲んだ nonda ② おいしい oishii　(2) ① 見た mita ② おもしろい omoshiroi

　(3) ① した shita ② 楽しい tanoshii

3.(1)読んだ, 読んで yonda, yonde　(2)飲んだ, 飲んで nonda, nonde

　(3)聞いた, 聞いて kiita, kiite

4.(1) ③　(2) ④　(3) ②

Lesson 15

Exercises

2. Examples:

　(1)わたしはイスラム教徒なので。　Watashi wa Isuramu-kyooto na node.

　(2) 大切なお祭りがあるので。Taisetsuna o-matsuri ga aru node.

　(3) ラマダンなので。Ramadan na node.

3.(1) 5 時に起きなければいけません 5-ji ni okinakereba ikemasen

　(2)薬を飲まなければいけません kusuri o nomanakereba ikemasen

　(3)帰らなければいけません kaeranakereba ikemasen

4.(1)牛肉を食べてはいけません gyuuniku o tabete wa ikemasen

　(2)たばこを吸ってはいけません tabako o sutte wa ikemasen

　(3)ごみを捨ててはいけません gomi o sutete wa ikemasen

6.(1)飲めます, 飲めません nomemasu, nomemasen

　(2)食べられます, 食べられません taberaremasu, taberaremasen

　(3)できます, できません dekimasu, dekimasen

Kana Index

194

197

Romanized Index

執筆者一覧
　　谷口すみ子　　　中央大学、津田塾大学非常勤講師
　　萬浪絵理　　　　㈶海外技術者研修協会　非常勤講師
　　稲子あゆみ　　　レコル・ドゥ・ジュネス　主催
　　萩原弘毅　　　　㈱スリーエーネットワーク

イラストレーション
　　佐藤夏枝
　　田辺澄美

カバーデザイン
　　小笠原博和

写真提供
　　郵政省

はじめのいっぽ
First Steps in Japanese

1995年 3月10日　初版第 1 刷発行
2004年 4月27日　第 11 刷 発 行

著　者　谷口すみ子　　萬 浪 絵 理
　　　　稲子あゆみ　　萩 原 弘 毅
発　行　株式会社　スリーエーネットワーク
　　　　〒101-0064 東京都千代田区猿楽町2-6-3（松栄ビル）
　　　　電話　営業　03(3292)5751
　　　　　　　編集　03(3292)6521
　　　　http://www.3anet.co.jp
印　刷　倉敷印刷株式会社

初級日本語教材の定番 みんなの日本語シリーズ

みんなの日本語初級 I

本冊	2,500円	標準問題集	900円
本冊・ローマ字版	2,500円	漢字英語版	1,800円
翻訳・文法解説ローマ字版（英語）	2,000円	漢字カードブック	600円
翻訳・文法解説英語版	2,000円	初級で読めるトピック25	1,400円
翻訳・文法解説中国語版	2,000円	書いて覚える文型練習帳	1,300円
翻訳・文法解説韓国語版	2,000円	漢字練習帳	900円
翻訳・文法解説スペイン語版	2,000円	教え方の手引き	2,800円
翻訳・文法解説フランス語版	2,000円	練習C・会話イラストシート	2,000円
翻訳・文法解説ポルトガル語版	2,000円	導入・練習イラスト集	2,200円
翻訳・文法解説タイ語版	2,000円	カセットテープ	6,000円
翻訳・文法解説インドネシア語版	2,000円	携帯用絵教材	6,000円
翻訳・文法解説ロシア語版	2,000円	B4サイズ絵教材	36,000円
翻訳・文法解説ドイツ語版	2,000円	会話ビデオ	10,000円

みんなの日本語初級 II

本冊	2,500円	標準問題集	900円
翻訳・文法解説英語版	2,000円	漢字英語版	1,800円
翻訳・文法解説中国語版	2,000円	初級で読めるトピック25	1,400円
翻訳・文法解説韓国語版	2,000円	書いて覚える文型練習帳	1,300円
翻訳・文法解説スペイン語版	2,000円	教え方の手引き	2,800円
翻訳・文法解説フランス語版	2,000円	練習C・会話イラストシート	2,000円
翻訳・文法解説ポルトガル語版	2,000円	カセットテープ	6,000円
翻訳・文法解説タイ語版	2,000円	携帯用絵教材	6,500円
翻訳・文法解説インドネシア語版	2,000円	B4サイズ絵教材	38,000円
翻訳・文法解説ロシア語版	2,000円	会話ビデオ	10,000円
翻訳・文法解説ドイツ語版	2,000円		

みんなの日本語初級　やさしい作文　1,200円

ホームページで
新刊や日本語セミナーを
ご案内しております
http://www.3anet.co.jp

価格は税別です　**スリーエー**ネットワーク

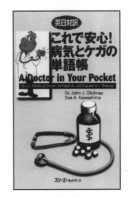